What I Saw When I Went Blind

by John H. Erickson

WESTBOW
P R E S S®
A DIVISION OF THOMAS NELSON
& ZONDERVAN

Edited and prepared for publication by Jessica Royer Ocken Oak Park, IL

Cover design by Mona Luan.
Cover concept by JP Erickson and Ellie Erickson

WestBow Press books may be ordered through booksellers or by contacting:

WestBow Press
A Division of Thomas Nelson & Zondervan
1663 Liberty Drive
Bloomington, IN 47403
www.westbowpress.com
1 (866) 928-1240

ISBN: 978-1-5127-1527-9 (sc)
ISBN: 978-1-5127-1528-6 (e)

Library of Congress Control Number: 2015916552

Print information available on the last page.

WestBow Press rev. date: 04/20/2016

Contents

I n the fall of 1972, I was 16 years old, and it appeared to most that I was near the end of my life.

I had required nine emergency surgeries over the last four years, each time to replace a plastic shunt on the right side of my neck that drained fluid to relieve pressure on my brain. The shunts each worked for a while, but they always failed in the end. That's why on February 2, 1972, I once again lay unconscious at Illinois Masonic Medical Center after a seizure.

My doctors didn't know why their efforts continued to fail, but they finally told my parents they were not able to replace the shunt again, and nothing more could be done. A priest arrived to administer my Last Rites.

But with nothing left to lose, my parents approved a last-ditch experimental technique—a high-risk procedure that would put a new shunt from my head down the back of my neck, right next to my spine. The risks of the surgery had not been worth the potential for disaster and failure until now. But my parents just wanted to buy me a little more time, if they could.

This is the story of how I became legally blind, and all the things I've seen since then that I would never have seen otherwise.

Chapter 1:   My First Life

GROWING UP IN MAYBERRY

I t all started in a safe, comfortable home in River Forest, Illinois—a small, residential, relatively affluent suburb to the west of Chicago. River Forest had a population of 12,000 people 50 years ago, and it's got 11,000 people now. This is not the result of people abandoning the village, but rather it's the result of people coming back to where they grew up, buying the older, smaller homes, and tearing them down to build larger ones. The village is full of people who grew up here a generation ago and have returned to bring up their own families. But all those families are smaller than they were 50 years ago!

It could be said that people from River Forest are a lot like salmon: they are born here, they leave to go to school and get a job, but they eventually come right back here to breed.

I am one of those salmon.

When I was growing up, River Forest truly seemed like the kind of place where Andy, Opie, and Aunt Bee would have felt right at home.

My family's first house was a cool tri-level home with three small bedrooms and a half-basement. I shared one of those bedrooms with my twin brother and best friend, Pete. When our two younger sisters, Karen and JoAnne, came along, they shared the other small bedroom, and my folks had their bedroom on the third level.

BUD AND THE BABE

When it comes to my mom and dad, Joan Carroll Erickson (known throughout her life as "the Babe") and Hubbard H. Erickson Jr. (who was known as "Bud"), I hit the proverbial Parent Jackpot. They are wonderful people.

Both my mom and dad were born in River Forest and lived most of their lives there. They attended Oak Park-River Forest High School in the 1940s.

My dad was 15 years old when Pearl Harbor was bombed and the United States entered World War II. As with many young men of his generation, going into the service right from high school was a no-brainer for him. As he tells it, he was not a very good student, and he might never have gotten out of high school if not for the war! My dad would tell us this whenever he wanted to commend us for good grades or console us when we were upset about getting a not-so-good grade.

My father enlisted in the Navy when he turned 17. Because of his love of flying, he went into aviation, where he eventually won his wings and was commissioned as a naval aviator. By the end of the war he had decided to make the Navy his career. Unfortunately, shortly thereafter my grandfather became seriously ill, and financial pressures forced my dad to leave active duty after 4 years. He transferred to a naval reserve squadron so he could continue to fly on weekends and come home to work with his father during the week to produce the Chicago National Boat Show, which my grandfather had founded in the early 1930s. After the boating industry came together to form a national trade association, which took over the show, my grandfather was able to retire and close his office.

For the next several years of my dad's working life, he and his partner managed the physical operations for many of the major trade shows and expositions at Navy Pier in downtown Chicago. Navy Pier at that time was nothing more than a warehouse, which had been abandoned by the Navy following the war, and my father actually had to live there in a converted office—often for weeks at a time—during major events. As the rapidly growing post-war trade show and convention industry began to blossom, my father went on to produce major industry events of his own at the request of some of the newly established trade associations, first in Chicago, then all over the United States, and eventually even overseas. He's now recognized as one of the founding fathers of the post-war trade show and convention industry in the United States.

My mom graduated from high school after WWII was over, and she went on to Marymount College in New York and got her teaching degree. She was teaching grade school in Oak Park when her cousin called to invite her to go bowling. Her cousin then called my dad and asked him to join them. My dad thought the other person coming along was just another guy, so he was very pleasantly surprised when the additional bowler turned out to be my mom.

They got married in August of 1955 and were living in a small River Forest apartment when they unexpectedly became the parents of twins, my brother Pete and me, the very next June. (The twins were the surprise, not becoming parents!) My sister Karen was born less than two years later in April 1958, so my folks had the dubious distinction of having two children on their first anniversary, two children on their second, three children on their third anniversary, and finally having more years married than children on their fourth anniversary. My dad told me once that back in 1960, having that many kids so soon after getting married had "raised some eyebrows!"

My mom retired from teaching just before Pete and I were born, and she was able to be a stay-at-home mom for all of us. In that role she always found time to be whatever was needed at our grade school: Cub Scout den mother, Girl Scout leader, picture lady, room mother, and PTA member. At the same time, my dad always found the time to be a Cub Scout leader and either a coach or manager of Pete's or my Little League team.

But I'm getting ahead of myself.

There's little doubt in my mind that my very first understanding of the world around me and my early definitions of right and wrong were formed as a toddler— the time when just about all communications between child and adult are dominated by "No!" My parents have told me several times that Pete and I were very active as infants, always playing off one another in both good and bad ways.

A typical example of this behavior was captured on film one day as Pete and I ate our lunch in our highchairs at my grandmother's house. Pete is looking right at the camera and putting a piece of food in his mouth. I'm sitting next to him, reaching over to his tray and taking food off his plate! My mother says Pete and I generally played well together, and she really didn't know at the time how full her hands were with us because we were her first experience with parenting.

4

Luckily for Pete and me, our dad was not quick to anger, nor was he a "yeller." He was, however, quick to pull us aside and in a very slow and deliberate tone—bordering on menacing—remind us of what was appropriate and inappropriate behavior. I'm sure this started when Pete and I were as young as three years old. As the lessons of appropriate behavior became clear to me, two basic precepts came into focus: good behavior is rewarded, and bad behavior leads to correction and sometimes punishment. I caught on to this pretty quickly.

As a preschooler, I had a great interest in the garbage men coming each week. During the nice-weather months, I made it a point to go out and see the garbage men come to our house in their big truck. I loved to watch them pour the garbage into the back of the truck and then see the powerful crusher devour it. My parents say the garbage men were the only ones to whom I would ultimately surrender the tattered remains of my baby blanket or "nonny," as baby blankets were called in my home. And the garbage men liked me too—one of them even gave me an 8x10 glossy photo of a brand new garbage truck one day. It was proudly displayed on my bedroom wall for several years.

I suspect it was because of this over-the-top interest in the garbage men that when Pete and I were about six, Dad took us out to the military museum at Cantigny in Winfield, Illinois. As long as I was so interested in heavy metal vehicles, I might as well know about the military as a career option—along with sanitary engineering. Well, once I saw my first tank, garbage trucks were kicked to the curb.

Not long after that, my father taught Pete and me how to build model planes and tanks. I was hooked.

by John H. Erickson

Next it was time to leave home for a bit and experience school. It became clear to me very quickly that the same rules applied at school as at home: good behavior is rewarded, and bad behavior is not. My first memory of being corrected at school was being sent to the Time Out rug in kindergarten for chasing another little boy around the room with a block I was pretending was a gun. My interest in guns was not shared or rewarded by most of my early educators.

And society as a whole was probably far safer for many years as a result of my sentence to the Time Out rug. This nip-it-in-the-bud action left me with a lasting message: not everyone shares my enthusiasm for military hardware and history. Still, the military and war were hugely fascinating to me, and those interests were a driving force throughout grade school. My daughter was fascinated one day to find old report cards of mine from second grade where the teacher had written, "John is very artistic but focuses only on drawing tanks and ships." The military remains an interest and hobby of mine today.

The grade school my siblings and I attended, Washington School, was just two and a half blocks away, and we did not have to cross a single busy street to get there. We walked to school, and it was like an an episode of *Leave it to Beaver* every day. Pete and I were good students and got basically identical grades—except that Pete always got an A in handwriting and I got a B, and I've realized since that even a B was an absolute gift. Although I loved to draw tanks and planes, writing was just about getting my ideas down on paper. How it looked wasn't important to me at all. And it looked atrocious!

Our good grades also put Pete and me in good standing

with our parents and grandparents. Both sets of my grandparents also lived in River Forest, less than one mile away from our house. Grampa Joe Carroll, my maternal grandfather, was such an outspoken supporter of good grades that he would often offer 25 cents for every A we got on a report card. This doesn't seem like much now, but at that time, Pete and I were getting 25 cents a week in allowance for doing our chores around the house like taking out the trash and keeping our room picked up. The prospect of getting a month or two of allowance for working a little harder to get As was well worth the effort!

When I was about eight years old, my Social Studies class at school studied the life of Helen Keller. I found her story remarkable, but it also haunted me as I saw in detail the hardships a person would face if he was totally blind. What if I had an accident and went blind too? I had always worn glasses because I was mildly nearsighted, but hearing the story of Helen Keller's life made me scared of being blind. What if the worst happened to me, and I lost my sight in an accident of some sort? Could I really live that way?

Being blind seemed to me the same as having both eyes closed: total darkness. I can remember being excused from the dinner table to go to the bathroom, which was on the second floor. On my way back to the dinner table, I would sometimes close my eyes as if I were blind and feel the walls of the house to help guide me back. I could not imagine what it would be like to be blind all the time. How would I go to school, play sports, find a job, and live any kind of normal life if I did not have my eyesight?

Being blind would be terrible! It would be scary, it would be frustrating, and it would be sad. I would only know someone was near if I could hear them talking to me. Goodbye independence. I would need help with everything, and lots of things would be impossible.

Just about everything the eight-year-old me liked to do used my eyesight—school, sports, drawing, and building models. It seemed that everything I knew about the world, and anything I would learn about the world in the future, would come to me through my eyes. If someone had asked me which of my five senses I thought was the most important, I most certainly would have said my eyesight. And I think most other people would feel the same way.

But as scary as those thoughts were, the idea of being blind had an even deeper negative implication in my young mind. The stories I knew about blind people from the Bible portrayed being blind as something that condemns you to the lowest levels of human existence. And the images of blind people in the Bible were even more graphic and sad than the life of Helen Keller. All the blind people mentioned in the Bible are beggars, with the only possible exception to this being Samson.

After Samson lost all his supernatural strength because he cut his hair off, he was blinded by his enemies, the Philistines, and chained inside their temple to be ridiculed. The Bible says Samson's hair eventually grew back, and he prayed for a final burst of strength, which allowed him to topple the main pillars of the temple. The whole structure collapsed, killing everyone inside, including him. If that was supposed to be a success story for a blind person, it did not sound very appealing to me.

Anyway, despite the rewards doing well in the classroom could afford us, doing well in gym class and other athletics was much more important to both Pete and me than school work was. In those first years of grade school, I was one of the taller boys in the class, and Pete was a couple inches shorter than me. In general, I was respectable in all sports, but Pete was a little faster and more talented.

We were the offensive ends of the Washington grade school football team, and at the pinnacle of our football career there was an end-around-with-a-pass play where Pete took the handoff from the running back and passed the football to me for a touchdown. My height helped me in basketball and volleyball, but kickball was my forte. I had a knack for punting the ball with great distance and accuracy, and I actually posted home runs while playing kickball inside the gym—one time by kicking the ball through the opposite basketball hoop, once by kicking it out the window of the gym, and a third time by wedging the ball between the roof and the rafters!

During the summers back in the 1960s, the only non-school sports program around in River Forest was Little League. It was for boys 7 to 12 years old and ran for about ten weeks. It was a great opportunity to become teammates with boys from other grade schools. I have great memories of playing Little League, and even a handful of memories of stellar performances on the field.

Not long ago, following a high school reunion, I was getting a ride home with Joe Barrett, a classmate from high school who had been one of the best baseball players in River Forest Little League during the years when Pete and I played. I was amazed when Joe asked me if I remembered "that amazing catch" I made in the outfield one time when he was batting.

I was delighted to tell him I did remember that catch, but I had to share my vantage point on the event. When Joe had come to the plate, everyone on our team had dropped back, including me in right field. We expected the ball to be hit sharply. And sure enough, a pitch or two later, Joe's bat cracked, and he sent a screaming line drive right toward me in right field. When he first hit the ball, I took a couple steps backward, fearing the worst, but then I saw that the ball was not going high into the air, so I started to charge, now fearing it was a "Texas leaguer" hit, and it would drop in front of me.

But after a few steps forward, I realized the hit was more of a "cruise missile" and the ball was about to career over my head, so I shot up my glove hand in sheer desperation! By the grace of God, I caught the ball and was so surprised at what had happened that I wasn't quite sure what to do next, at least for a split second or two. Apparently, spectators saw the play as a fine defensive reaction in the outfield rather than, as I saw it, a close call and near humiliation of epic proportions!

Pete and I wrapped up our Little League careers in the summer between sixth and seventh grade, but that wasn't the only activity we enjoyed together. Our dad always made sure there were plenty of things for us to do at home. When he wasn't working at his office, Dad was working around the house—mowing the lawn in the summer or building an ice skating rink in the backyard during the winter. This was so cool to us because not only could we skate in our own backyard, but lots of kids from the neighborhood came to our house to skate too! Dad managed this while running his own company and flying around the country to produce trade shows and conventions.

Despite all our sports activities and general roughhousing with each other, Pete and I suffered no real serious injuries growing up. Pete got frostbite one winter because he stayed out too long skating in the backyard, and I did have a history of banging my head and getting stitches—once falling off a fence while climbing between backyards, once racing with

Pete through the house and hitting the TV instead of the couch, and once getting hit accidentally by a friend with a broom. (No, really, it was an accident!)

However, there was one other malady I suffered growing up. Once in a while, when I stayed up past my normal bedtime, I would experience very uncomfortable shocks or shooting pains in my legs. These weren't a problem during the school year, as I kept a very regular bedtime schedule, but this problem did occur during long summer nights and on occasional weekends when Pete and I slept over at a friend's house.

I don't ever remember talking to a doctor or my folks about my leg problem because it wasn't a chronic thing. When it did occur, I simply called it quits for the night, went to bed, and tried to fall asleep as quickly as possible. Luckily for the general reputation of the Erickson twins, Pete was a night owl and could stay up and party with the most nocturnal of our friends.

THE COTTAGE IN MICHIGAN

Because he had his own business, Dad realized very early in his marriage that there never were going to be two- or three-week family vacations because he had to be available at the office all year round. So he bought some wooded property in Michigan on the shore of Lake Michigan, just over two hours away from our home, where we would vacation almost every weekend during the summer after Little League was done. We camped out there for the first time the summer when Pete and I were six, Karen was four, and our sister JoAnne was just an infant, having been born that very summer of 1962. (I think now that my parents were very gutsy to camp with so many small children.) Dad built a simple but adequate and functional cottage there the next summer, and he worked each weekend we were there to slowly improve it, summer after summer.

Occasionally, this meant Pete and I were called upon to help with things like moving railroad ties or piles of sand and dirt from here to there, and crawling under the house to turn the water on and off, which was our favorite. (Not!) In between these occasional chores, there were days and days of playing on the beach, in the water, and my favorite: Pete and I hunting each other down in the woods with our toy machine guns!

And there was another reason we all enjoyed going to the cottage in Michigan: the Kettlehut family. Just a year or two after we started vacationing there, a childhood friend of my mom's, Bill Kettlehut, bought property down the beach from our cottage, and the Kettlehut family began making regular trips to Michigan just like us. There were also four children in their family: Billy, Susan, Betsy, and Nancy. Susan was a year older than Pete and me, while Betsy was a year younger. Billy was three years older, and Nancy was three years younger.

When Pete and I were about ten, I think, we still regularly enjoyed playing army in the woods. But soon after that we realized there were really cute girls just down the beach—and they were wearing swimming suits! After that, doing just about anything with the Kettlehuts was more fun than playing army!

But we couldn't keep them a secret from our other friends for long. Whereas friends used to always say, "Yes, sure!" when we asked them to come to the cottage for a weekend with us, they now started to say, "Well, will the Kettlehuts be up there too?"

Seeing Susan, Betsy, Bill, and Nancy almost every time we

went to the cottage became a regular part of our time there. The Kettlehuts taught us all how to waterski when Billy was old enough to drive the motorboat, and Pete and I always called Susan, Betsy, and Nancy when we collected firewood to have a fire on the beach, which was almost every weekend. They always brought graham crackers, chocolate bars, and marshmallows to make the S'mores.

For our tenth birthday, Pete and I received a ten-foot Styrofoam sail boat called The Snark. (Note: Getting joint or shared gifts for birthdays comes with the territory when you are a twin.) Dad taught the two of us the fundamentals of sailing on Lake Michigan. And even though he added a fiberglass coating to the hull of the boat, the rigors of having two boys crashing it in the surf resulted in The Snark cracking in half two years later.

By that time, sailing had become one of our favorite things to do, so with some help from our parents, Pete and I saved up, pooled our money, and bought a new Sunfish to continue our sailing adventures.

MY TWO LIVES

Another huge interest I had as a young boy was James Bond, Agent 007. The first of the James Bond movies, *Dr. No*, was released in 1962, when I was six years old. By the time the fifth James Bond movie, *You Only Live Twice*, was released in 1967, I had seen each of the previous four at least once, as well as watching every TV special about anything having to do with 007. I also had my own James Bond attaché case, possessed several toy replicas of the Astin Martin DB5, and had collected the soundtracks to all of the movies.

And as I prepared for junior high, I was about to discover

that the theme song from *You Only Live Twice* was particularly relevant to my life. Things were about to change dramatically for me. I would soon begin my second life.

At the end of the summer of 1968, when it was time to go to seventh grade, this meant a move to River Forest Junior High. This was a momentous progression for Pete and me, but the junior high stood adjacent to the new grade school, so travel plans were same as before.

Junior high brought on a lot of changes, and for me, most of them were bad. The most noticeable and important to me at that time was that I lost my rather high physical status versus my fellow male peers. I had enjoyed quite a bit of popularity in elementary school, probably due to being "one of the twins" and one of the tallest kids in the class. Pete and I had many times been elected squad leaders in gym class, which was a big deal to me.

But when seventh grade rolled around, within what seemed like a matter of months, other boys morphed into superior specimens of male adolescence. In contrast, during that first semester of seventh grade, I noticed a significant decline in my athletic performance. When I played football that fall, I no longer dominated other players, which was very disheartening.

And maybe even more troubling to me, I no longer felt I was pleasing the gym teachers with my performance. One time in early seventh grade, I was trying to put a positive spin on my now average physique by mentioning how light I was to my new gym teacher. He replied, "Well, muscle weighs more than fat." I don't think I was being oversensitive to take that as a cut.

At the same time, I also began to slip from the higher scholastic tier I had enjoyed throughout grade school. My seventh grade grades fell from mostly As and an occasional B to Bs and Cs. I found each class far more challenging than any I had experienced before.

I did not complain to my folks about most of these things because they seemed in no position to solve my problems. If my grades were falling, I had to work harder. If I was no longer a good athlete, maybe my time of such glory was just over, and I had to come to grips with that. But my self-esteem took a real hit during seventh grade. And on top of all that, I had begun having frequent headaches, as well as a dramatic flare-up in the number of leg-pain attacks I experienced—and during the school year now, not just when I stayed up too late in the summer.

These symptoms finally got bad enough that I did mention them to my parents, who promptly took me to see our family doctor. During that doctor's visit, I remember mentioning not just the headaches but also the advent of "mobility problems," as I think I called them, because calling it "weird clumsiness" didn't seem very medical.

My doctor chalked up my complaints to the stress of junior high—a very reasonable diagnosis at the time, as I saw it. However, he did not have any explanation or suggested remedy for my leg problem, the uncomfortable "shocks" I was feeling in my legs at night.

FURTHER DIAGNOSIS

I continued my schoolwork and struggled to adjust to my new place in the social status of junior high, but early during the second semester of seventh grade, I found myself back at the doctor. I'd suddenly noticed that the words on the chalkboard were very blurry. If I removed my glasses, the

by John H. Erickson

words were clearer for a few moments, but my eyes would soon start to hurt. Presuming that a new prescription for my glasses was in order, my mom scheduled the next available appointment for me with my eye doctor, which was right after school the following week. It was February of 1969.

During his initial examination, the doctor was very concerned to find that I had lost 25% of my vision in one eye and 40% in the other. He did not have an explanation for such a loss and recommended that my mom immediately take me over to the local hospital to determine the nature of the problem.

I don't recall being alarmed at the prospect of going to the hospital for further testing, because the hospital had always done a good job of patching me up when I needed stitches. Those visits had all been very short ones—I had never stayed overnight there. I figured this visit was going to be just the same, so I wasn't scared. After all, I wasn't a kid anymore. I was 12 and a half—practically a teenager! I definitely didn't want to show any fear or concern about what was going on—that's what little boys do. Besides, I figured it would be impossible to stay at the hospital for too long. I had school the next day.

I remember feeling confident that, finally, someone had diagnosed a real problem, and we were on the verge of discovering the source of my failing eyesight, and maybe a couple of my other problems: the serious headaches, the tripping and stumbling on stairs and sidewalks, and the increased twitching and pain in my legs. Maybe we were on our way to fixing it all!

So we left the eye doctor and drove to West Suburban Hospital. My mom told the front desk why we were there, and I was a bit surprised when she told me the hospital was going to check me in.

I kept up my strong front because it was just Mom with me at the time. I remember that Dad was dealing with a very serious crisis at work. Just a couple months earlier, he'd been setting up a show at McCormick Place, Chicago's premier and relatively new convention center, when the building caught fire and burned to the ground. Since then, Dad had spent many, many nights downtown looking for another location for his show, hoping to save it. When Mom called to tell him she was checking me in at the hospital for the night, he had already been working through one disaster, and now there might be another one about to land on my parents' plate.

THE INPATIENT EXPERIENCE

Over the years, many people have asked how I felt during those first days in the hospital. There were many emotions to deal with for my twelve-year-old self, but the ones I remember most clearly are impatience and frustration.

Surprisingly, as I think back, there was little fear during those early days. My eyesight seemed to me to be something that could be easily fixed—maybe with some kind of quick operation. Though I was bored and annoyed at my situation, I remained rather calm about things.

After all, my parents seemed calm, and I just assumed they had a much better handle on what was going on than I did. If they were not panicking, I wasn't going to panic either. Both my mom and dad spoke to me without indication of fear or indecision. But I know now that's not how they felt on the inside. Years later my dad told me they'd been as clueless about what was happening as I was, and they'd been very scared and concerned. But they chose to stay positive on the outside—and that's just what I wanted and needed to see.

by John H. Erickson

After checking into the hospital, I had expected to take a battery of tests and have the doctors figure out quickly what the problem was. I had the utmost confidence that they would then move on to fixing what was ailing me. But, on the contrary, time seemed to slow down after I got to the hospital.

No private rooms were available when I checked in, so I was put in a room with two other boys, both several years younger than me. I don't know why either of them was there, because neither one of them said a word to me when I moved into the room, nor over the next several days. I didn't try to start a conversation with them either, because I worried that maybe they were in a lot of pain and not in the mood to talk. And I still thought I was only going to be there a day or two.

I remember that each of them had their own TV set, but I did not, and neither one of them asked me if there was anything I wanted to watch. The TVs were at the far end of the room anyway, so I couldn't see the screens clearly. So, during the day, both the TVs were on but not tuned to any channel I was interested in, and not positioned so I could see them.

One time, when one of the other boys left his bed for a test or something, I went and sat on his bed to see his TV better. When the boy came back to our room with the nurse, she scolded me for leaving my bed and getting into his. It didn't seem like any big deal to me, but she was quite emphatic that I never do it again.

After that I just laid in my bed, day after day, waiting for the next test. I was very impatient that things weren't moving along any quicker, and it was frustrating not having something to do.

With three beds in the one room, there was very little space for any of us to have visitors. There were no curtains to pull across to make your area a bit more private, so my parents were the only ones who stopped by to visit, and they only stayed a very short time. The person who I would have liked to come more than anyone, Pete, was too young to visit that part of the hospital.

Other than the one who'd scolded me, the nurses seemed nice enough, but I don't remember any of them striking up any kind of meaningful conversation with me.

I did, however, cross paths with someone who seemed as impatient and frustrated with me as I was with the hospital. I left my room one morning for an EEG, an electroencephalogram. For this test, the technician pasted sensors to different parts of my head, I lay on a gurney, and I was told to stay very still while the technician monitored my brain waves.

This did not sound difficult when the technician explained it, and I was confident I could complete the test. I tried to relax and do exactly what he had told me, but one of my legs had other ideas. As I lay there, I suddenly felt a sensation like someone had touched the tip of my toe with a live wire connected to a car battery. It was that same sensation that had plagued me for many years as my nighttime leg problem. Lately it had been hitting me more often, and not always at night.

I felt my leg twitch, and the technician said, "Stay still." I said I was sorry, took a deep breath, and focused on keeping my leg still. But ten seconds later, the twitch struck again.

"I said keep still!" the technician said, in a very annoyed voice this time.

No one had ever told me what to call this sensation in my leg, so I tried to explain. "It's my leg," I said. "I can't keep it still. I think it's the lack of exercise." I had no other excuse to use.

The technician said nothing, so I tightened up all the muscles in my legs and braced for the next twitch. When it came, my leg still shook, even as I tried to hold it still. There was nothing I could do about it.

"I said, stay still!" the technician barked. He must have left his desk and come over to where I was because the next thing I felt was something pricking the bottom of my bare foot. The technician said, "Do you feel that? Now stay still!" He was downright mad at me!

We tried the test one more time, but it was no use. My leg twitched, and the technician ended the EEG. I was taken back to my room, and I never told anyone about the incident. As I saw it, I had blown the test. I hadn't done what I was told to do, though I still didn't know why I couldn't do it.

No one ever told me anything about the results of the test, or even whether it had actually been completed. And I wasn't about to ask about it, because I did not want to be thrown back with that technician again!

I was at West Suburban Hospital in neighboring Oak Park for seven days.

Eventually, the doctors said they suspected some kind of pressure around my optic nerve was responsible for the loss of sight, and probably the other maladies too: the headaches, the stumbling, the increase in the leg pains, and maybe even my declining grades and poor sports performance. So my dad and mom packed up my hospital room one day and drove me to Illinois Masonic Medical Center—a bigger hospital in downtown Chicago, about 11 miles away, that was known for its experts in neurology.

It was there that Dr. Ronald Pawl came into my life. Dr. Pawl was a neurosurgeon at Masonic and would become the man who literally saved my life nine times in the next three years. He had a great bedside manner. Like my dad, he spoke with confidence and authority, and I found it easy to put my trust in him.

Fortunately, we were able to get a private room right away at the new hospital, and this allowed one of my folks to be with me most of the time. I also remember the hospital staff at Masonic as much friendlier, very polite and courteous. The nurses always had smiles on their faces when they came in and out of the room, although they were often difficult to understand. Many of them were Filipino.

Things were much busier at Masonic than they had been at the local hospital. I took many more trips out of the room for various tests. This kept me more entertained, but rather quickly, the tests became more invasive and challenging. The most memorable and painful were not one, but two, spinal taps.

Those tests began with me sitting backwards on a collapsible chair. I was dressed in one of those fetching hospital gowns that seemed totally open and tied in the back. I also didn't like the fact that there seemed to be a whole audience of resident doctors and nurses along with Dr. Pawl in the room during the procedure!

First they gave me a shot of local anesthetic right in the center of my back, which stung. Then, after a minute or so to give the anesthetic time to work, a bigger needle was inserted into my spine and a sample of cerebral fluid drawn out. Despite the anesthetic, the feeling was very, very uncomfortable.

While the procedure was going on, I remember thinking, *what does the fluid in my back have to do with my eyesight?* But, I did find out later that Dr. Pawl and his associate Dr. Sugar had done many studies and procedures having to do with pressure on the brain. They'd found that such pressure actually changes the color of one's cerebral fluid, and this is what they were checking on me.

I don't remember anyone talking to me about the doctors' final diagnosis, but I know now that they determined I was suffering from aqueductal stenosis. Everyone's brain produces cerebral fluid, and that fluid regularly drains from the head into the chest cavity, where it is reabsorbed into the body. For some reason (which was never discovered), my fluid had stopped draining, and the subsequent pressure it produced had manifested itself first as headaches, then as mobility problems, and finally with loss of vision as my optic nerves were damaged.

The spinal taps had provided the conclusive evidence that such pressure existed, and the treatment would be implanting a small plastic tube called a shunt to act as a bypass around the not-working drainage ventricle.

So, one morning I left my hospital room for what I thought was one more test, but instead was a surgery to put the shunt in. I woke up many hours later in the intensive care unit. I felt very weak, and there were all kinds of tubes going in and out of my body. I had also a lot of discomfort on the right side of my head and neck, and all my hair had been shaved off! My eyesight was also a lot worse than it had been before. I could tell there were hospital people walking around, but I couldn't see who they were.

Some time later, I returned to my own hospital room. My parents were there, and they explained the operation to me. After a general anesthetic, Dr. Pawl and the other doctors had shaved all the hair off my head and made an incision to peel back my scalp. They'd then drilled a hole through my skull into the area where the cerebral fluid was trapped, and they covered that hole with a plastic bubble. They attached a plastic shunt to that bubble and then ran the tube down my neck into my chest cavity. To do this, they had cut a long incision down my neck and behind my ear, and then made a one-inch incision in my chest so they could pull the end of the shunt into place.

That's why I now had bandages all the way from my chest, up my neck, and covering the right side of my head. I had not seen this coming at all! All that time I was wishing the doctors would find out what was wrong and fix it, I had imagined them removing a cataract or something.

My parents said I should rest until it was time to go home. I don't remember anyone specifically telling me a prognosis of what was to come, but I had lots of time to think about it over the next several days.

I did a lot of thinking because there wasn't much else I could do. I could hear the TV, but I could no longer see the screen. Words on paper were now too blurry to read, so there were no comic books or *Mad* magazines. I couldn't even draw, which had been one of my favorite pastimes, because I couldn't see a pencil line on paper. This was the beginning, though, of my appreciation of the radio.

All of these realizations made me think about sports. Baseball, basketball, and volleyball would be impossible with my newly reduced level of sight. Kickball, my favorite, was out too. I thought I could probably still kick the ball, but how would I run to the bases if I couldn't see them? And then, of course, there was school to think about. What was I going to do about reading all those books? How would I take notes in class if I couldn't see the blackboard? How would I take notes if I couldn't see the lines on the notebook paper? I didn't like feeling so helpless. I felt powerless, as though all my talents and abilities had been sucked out of me.

by John H. Erickson

But all my fears were immediate. I don't remember worrying about being visually impaired to any degree for the rest of my life. I wanted to believe that the doctors had simply identified the cause of my sight loss and taken the correct steps to clear the whole thing up, although it might take many months to do so.

During one of my few visits back to the junior high in seventh grade to see teachers, one of them asked me, "Do they expect your eyes to get better again?"

"Oh, yes," I answered. "If they keep the pressure off the optic nerve, the eyesight should come back."

But no one had ever told me that. It was the wishful prognosis of a twelve-year-old imagination, but it seemed very reasonable. My eyesight had not failed all of a sudden; it had slowly, almost imperceptibly gotten worse. So it seemed logical that the damaged tissues would heal if they were given the chance. I did not know then that brain tissue, which includes the optic nerves, never regenerates naturally after it's been damaged.

I do remember in eighth grade, when my eyesight had still not improved, asking my Dad, "What are we going to do when it's time for me to start driving or get a job?"

"We're not going to worry about that right now," he said. "We just need to figure out how to get your books read for next semester."

Well, okay. I understood the need to work harder right now to do school work, and I was okay with that, but no one had any answers about how to get back all the fun things in my life! This did not make me feel good.

So I consumed myself with solving short-term challenges, not contemplating the really bad what-ifs of the future. It wasn't denial exactly, but it accomplished the same thing: I didn't let myself mourn the loss of my sight and the life with good eyesight I'd once known. I also didn't think much about the new emotions being visually handicapped might bring. There was, of course, the frustration and impatience I'd felt during my days and weeks in the hospital, but I counted on the belief that those times would eventually end.

The emotion I did not see coming (no pun intended) was loneliness, but it's been an on-and-off again companion since I was twelve.

Chapter 2:   A New Way of Life

THE FAMILY I HAD NOT APPRECIATED

'll never forget the day I came home from the hospital after my first shunt-implantation operation. I had been gone for about two and a half weeks, and I was still recovering from the surgery. I was on some pretty great painkillers when my dad brought me through the front door of the house.

As he did, my mom and all of my siblings were right there to welcome me. I was delighted that everyone had set aside their busy schedules to greet me. Then I saw the banner! My brother and sisters had made a sign that stretched almost across the whole living room, and it said "Welcome Home, John!" I was truly amazed. They had really missed me!

Before my first surgery, I would have classified our family life as maybe a little better than average. There were no huge conflicts, mostly because any serious arguments were quickly quelled by my father, who made it clear that he did not want openly negative interactions around the house. As a result, Pete and I pretty much lived our lives as the twins, while Karen and JoAnne lived their lives, avoiding too much interference and conflict with each other. This seemed to change for the better after this first of many trips to the hospital. All four of us siblings seemed to interact more and have a good time together. For the next three months, I continued to recover, and everyone in my family pitched in to help.

After I came home from that first hospital stay, with severe sight loss and lots of discomfort from the surgery, my biggest immediate concern was my physical appearance. Not only was all my hair gone, but there were bandages up and down my neck. Plus I was on some kind of medication that caused me to retain water and made me bloated. I was very disturbed that I now looked fat. I remember being very self-conscious when a small group of girls from school stopped by my house to say hi.

I never went back to classes that second semester of seventh grade. For three months following the operation, my mom drove me back to Masonic each day for a radiation zap. This was a precautionary move the doctors wanted, based on the small chance of an undiscovered tumor in the problem area. When those treatments were completed each day, we launched into trying to get me caught up with my classes at school. My mom read me the books and assignments, some tutors came to the house each day, and we worked out modified final exams for my classes so I could resume school in the fall, still in the eighth grade with Pete and my other classmates.

ME VS. THE WHITE CANE

During the summer following my first operation, my father made plans for a mobility trainer from Hines Veterans Hospital to come to our house and teach me how to use a white cane. I remember objecting quite vigorously, saying, "Sure, Dad, I

By John H. Erickson

have some blurry eyesight now, but I don't need to have a white cane, for heaven's sake. I'm not blind!"

Luckily for me, my dad set up the instructor anyway, and I took my lessons. I could only protest so much. If my Dad felt strongly about something—and he did about this—I did it. He knew my eyesight was not coming back, but I still wasn't ready to accept that.

The lessons only took a week, and the instructor came to our home. I remember him as all-business and very little personality. We never really connected, and he wasn't someone I particularly wanted to please. But fortunately the training took only a few days, and I was able to pick up the skills I needed. I started training on the quiet sidewalks in River Forest around our house and progressed to the very busy intersection of Harlem and Lake Street just four blocks away. When we'd finished, I did know more about crossing a busy street, of which there were many near my home. But for many years, I kept my cane folded up and concealed as best I could most of the time.

When I made plans to venture outside the house, I just thought I'd do it the way I always had: mostly with Pete at my side. The last thing I wanted in my hand was a white cane. Walking and biking all around River Forest and nearby Oak Park had been a way of life for Pete and me. Within just five blocks of our house was school, two ice cream and burger places, many of our friends, a drug store, and a hardware store, among other things.

Though I'd never have said so at the time, I thought the white cane was a surrender of sorts, a surrender of independence and confidence. And it felt like a plea for pity. In fact, I once called it a "sympathy stick" when describing it to my friends.

It was my explanation for why I started to get such nice and preferred treatment from teachers and staff during eighth grade. In fact, during lunch at the junior high, my friends would ask me to go back to the food line with their plate and get more mashed potatoes. One woman working there always gave me two scoops, instead of the standard one, when I came to the line with my white cane in hand!

But as an adolescent boy, sympathy was the last thing I wanted. And I didn't want to call attention to myself either. Like most kids my age, I just wanted to fit in with everyone else, not stand out from the crowd. Because I had some sight, and consciously tried to look right at people when I spoke to them, there were very few outward clues that I was visually impaired. But the white cane blew my cover right away. So it was a long and often embarrassing road for me until I finally got with the white cane program several years down the line.

Looking back, I know I made things harder for myself over and over again. Many, many times I found myself at a familiar place like a restaurant or department store and had to go to the men's room. I'd ask and find out that it was "just down the hallway." That would sound easy, so I'd head that way without my cane. But when I arrived, I'd find two doors and not be able to tell which one was the men's room and which one was the ladies' room because I couldn't see well enough to read the signs.

So I'd ask the next person walking by which door was the men's room, and he'd say something like, "Oh, this door with the big sign saying *men's room* is the men's room."

Realizing how stupid the question must have sounded, I'd mutter some apology and realize if I had brought my cane along there would have been no question as to why I was asking. And then a few days or weeks later, I'd find myself in the same situation again.

My dad did not understand my reluctance to use the cane. He said the white cane seemed like a magic wand after he saw how people scurried to get out of my way when I had it. He saw it as a ticket to independence. But maybe another reason I didn't want to use a white cane was because I didn't like the idea of sporting a wand of any type. It made me sound like somebody's Fairy Godmother, or Tinker Bell!

"WHY CAN'T I DO THAT?"

Also that summer, I lamented that my sailing days were over because of my sight loss. But my dad said, "Why can't you sail? You're not at a greater disadvantage. No one else can see the wind either."

I don't think he was trying to be particularly profound or philosophical, but those words were exactly the wisdom I needed to hear. It would have been so easy to just write off sailing because of my eyesight, and no one would have argued. Instead, I embraced it and became the sailing expert in my family. I even joined the sailing club in college and crewed during some real regatta races. It wasn't that I was a great sailor—it was that I was scrawny and light, and I didn't cry when the captain yelled at me!

Today I continue to sail on Lake Michigan when we vacation there in the summer. It's one of my most favorite things to do. I've even found technology to fill my need for a live crew member because I can't see my way back to the beach near our cottage. I now have a talking GPS that speaks to me every 15 seconds and tells me how far I am from the shore and what direction our beach is from my boat.

That summer, Pete, my dad, and I also went to the bicycle store and bought a new tandem. For the next five years, Pete would be the driver of our tandem as we rode back and forth to school. What should be noted is that Pete gave up the use of a brand new five-speed bicycle he'd gotten just the summer before for his birthday. He had the cool sports car of bikes, but he was suddenly thrust into the role of bus driver for his twin brother. He never grumbled or complained once to me about this new responsibility. The tandem was the only bike of its type at the River Forest Junior High, and it made us sort of celebrities. But even then I knew what a huge favor Pete was doing for me.

That summer was also the first time my shunt failed. One morning, my family had great difficulty waking me up. When I finally responded, I acted like I was in some kind of drugged-out state. They popped me in the car and rushed up to Illinois Masonic Medical Center where Dr. Pawl removed the first shunt and put in another one.

It wasn't until this happened—when I woke up in the hospital with more eyesight loss and discovered the operation to put in the shunt and relieve the pressure on my brain had failed—that I realized my sight might remain impaired for many years to come. I was depressed, but I didn't ask anyone about my prognosis. I consciously chose to not consider the possibility that my eyesight was gone forever. I still needed some time to get my arms around where I was right now.

Ultimately, my eyesight would never get better. I was now a visually impaired person (VIP). And, unfortunately, the shunt would fail many more times over the next couple of years. The details are a little fuzzy to me, but I do know my memories of these times and my parents' memories are a bit different. As we've tried to recount these experiences over the years, I've realized that my parents remember from the perspective of those expected to protect their child from harm and pain. And in instances when that's not possible, they're supposed to do whatever they can to solve the problem. But in my case, my parents could do neither.

A couple times, we were vacationing in Michigan when a seizure occurred, and my dad had some interesting encounters with the state police as he sped back to the hospital two hours away. One time we were pulled over by a state trooper, but when my dad told him we were on the way to the emergency room, and the trooper saw my mom holding me in the backseat, he turned on his lights and siren and led my dad the rest of the way to the hospital—at well over 90 miles an hour!

Each time I would be rushed into the operating room to have one shunt cut out of my neck and a replacement shunt put in. Each time my eyesight got worse, and it was unclear whether I would survive the operation at all. The doctors told my parents they did not know why the shunts were failing. Although it was risky, taking out the old one and replacing it was the only option they had. Then I would wake up, and everyone would wait to see how much additional eyesight I had lost.

This was obviously extremely stressful for my parents, but from my vantage point, it was more an unpleasant recurring surprise. I would go to bed just fine, like any normal night. Then when I woke up, I would be in the intensive care unit of the hospital again. (It was like a bad version of Bill Murray in *Groundhog Day!*) The surroundings were vaguely familiar, I'd have lots of unexplained pain and discomfort, and lots of strangers milled around. One of my most vivid memories is my mom or dad putting cold washcloths on my forehead to ease the pain.

But probably most unsettling, all the hair on my head would be gone each time! I consider myself a lucky man that I had grandfathers with thick heads of hair and good genes. My hair just kept growing back.

RETURNING TO SCHOOL

When I returned to junior high at the start of eighth grade, Pete and I had all the same classes. Unfortunately, I was not in class very much because my shunt failed three times during my eighth grade year. I tried a couple of times to return, but most of my schoolwork that year was done at home with the help of my mom and tutors. When I was at school, I was still getting used to my very blurry vision, so my movements around the building were slow and tentative. But at least I was familiar with the hallways because I had been there for one semester the year before.

I realized the loneliness of being visually impaired during those first days in the eighth grade at River Forest Junior High. There were only a few times when Pete wasn't with me, but when he wasn't, I was surprised to feel so isolated.

It didn't make sense. Here I was with dozens and dozens of people walking around me, and they were all people I knew— some had been my friends since I started grade school. But now, I realized, I could not recognize anyone. I couldn't catch someone's eye and give a wave or smile. I couldn't spot a friend or two and join in their conversation. Occasionally, I would hear someone say hi or even "Hi, John!" But in the crowded hallway I couldn't be sure they were talking to me.

by John H. Erickson

I would just try to smile and say "hi" or "hey there" as I made my way to the next class. And that had challenges of its own.

On my initial class assignment sheet, the rooms were identified by number. Unfortunately, room numbers on the classes themselves were at the top of the door jamb—way too far away for me to see or feel with my hands. Luckily for me, River Forest Junior High had only two floors, with about ten classroom on each floor. Teachers had the same room year after year, so it was common knowledge where most classes met, and I was able to find my way around pretty well.

I can't say that I noticed any big change in the behavior of my friends when I returned to school. But then again, I didn't expect any big change. Eighth-grade boys are not generally known for a lot of "touchy feely" displays of compassion. I myself was trying all the time to display strength and toughness, and I didn't expect anything different from my friends and acquaintances. The stand-out exception to this was Pete. He made a huge effort every day to assist with whatever I needed. Ironically, this could have been a reason why others didn't see the need to step forward and help too.

I remember one time sitting with a classmate who asked me how I was reading my books. I told him my books were read to me by my mom or played on reel-to-reel tape so I could listen to them. "Oh, you're lucky!" he exclaimed. "I wish I could just listen to my books."

I didn't say anything, but I wanted to tell him it wasn't as great as it sounded. Listening to my textbooks on tape took twice as long as it would have if I could read the book. And I found out very quickly that there was no way to recline comfortably and listen to a textbook without falling dead asleep! I would have to rewind the tape again and again until I found the last section I remembered hearing, then play the whole thing over again. This added even more time to my homework assignments.

Another time I sat talking with a classmate when I noticed he was consistently shifting his head and body to the left as I talked to him. After several minutes of this behavior, I asked, "Why do you keep shifting to your left while we're talking?"

"Oh," he said, "that's because you keep looking over to my left. I'm just trying to get in to your line of sight."

Only then did it dawn on me that because all of my remaining sight was peripheral, in the left corner of my left eye, I turned my head to the right when talking to someone so I could best focus on them. From their view point, though, I appeared to be looking to their left, not at them. Great! All this time I've not been looking at people. That would be one more thing I had to compensate for when interacting with others.

And it has been, but I've since developed a system: When I talk with someone, I first glance at them out of the corner of my eye to find where their face is. Then I point my head at that spot and try to look there, even though that puts their face right in the middle of my blind spot. I know this makes others more comfortable, and it makes me appear more attentive to what they are saying. I do this with absolutely everyone, and I do it now without even thinking.

BRAILLE: AN OLD SKILL WORTH LEARNING

Despite all the coping mechanisms I had in place, my eighth grade teachers realized I needed to learn Braille in order to continue successfully with my education. It was arranged that I would go twice a week by cab from the River Forest Junior High to a grade school in Berwyn. This is where Mrs. Palmer taught me how to read and write Braille.

by John H. Erickson

The process was slow. Each Braille cell consists of six raised dots. Which of the six dots are raised in any particular cell tells you what letter or symbol (like a contraction or punctuation mark) that cell represents. At first, my finger would have to circle the cell over and over until I could perceive which dots were raised. Then, slowly, my fingers got more sensitive, and the Braille cells became more clear. After that it was a matter of memorizing each cell's meaning—truly like learning to read all over again.

By the time I left Mrs. Palmer, I could read a page of the Braille, but not much faster than a second grader reads print. Nevertheless, I thought of this as a huge accomplishment. I used Braille for the rest of my academic career, all during the 35 years of my working career, and I use it all the time now that I'm retired. I'm not a "fast" Braille reader, but I don't have to be, it just does a great job of keeping my life in order!

PUTTING LOSS IN PERSPECTIVE

Despite the major leap of learning Braille, the most meaningful thing that happened to me at that school in Berwyn was meeting John and Carolyn Novotny. John was just a year younger than I was, and Carolyn was a couple years younger than him. The Novotnys were smart, they were fun, and they were just as friendly as I was. The difference was they had both been born without eyes.

Long before grade school, they had been fitted with glass eyes and never seemed uncomfortable about their appearance or lack of eyesight. I thought about all that I'd enjoyed in my early years (my first life): playing sports and games and finding school pretty easy. After meeting John and Carolyn, I realized they'd never had any of those experiences, and it made me ashamed that I'd thought of my blurred vision as some kind of big deal. As the adage goes, I felt sorry for myself because I had no shoes until I met a man who had no feet. In this case, I felt sorry for myself because my eyesight was blurred, until I met two friends who had no eyes.

I started to recognize how lucky I was to still have some sight. More importantly, I realized that if I'd been born a decade or two earlier, I would probably be dead because the technology that saved my life would not have been invented yet!

It began to dawn on me what an enormous blessing my parents and siblings were too, and especially my twin brother. It's fair to say I had never before fully appreciated the fact that each and every day of my life was spent in the companionship of a best friend. We did Cub Scouts together. We did six years of Little League together. We went to church and Sunday School together, and we served as altar boys together. In sixth grade, when we were the defensive ends of the football team, the coach had nicknamed us his "Nordic bookends."

I had never been at a strange place with no one to play with—Pete was always there. There was never a time when I felt picked on or singled out for chores around the house—because Pete always had to do them with me. There was never a night when I had to go to bed by myself in a dark, scary room—Pete was always there having to do the same. And now I had a companion with me to face all the new challenges and changes that were to come.

Also, about a year after my first operation, our family expanded when my third sister, Mary Christine, was born in December 1969. I did not remember much about Karen and JoAnne being born and growing up, so I found MC's birth a fun and unique experience. Her arrival also seemed to finally take everyone's focus off of me! I was glad for this because I was tired of the spotlight it seemed people thought they had to keep on me.

CONNECTING WITH THE CANE

Over time, my feelings about the collapsible white cane did begin to change. The first experience I can remember that really demonstrated the power of the white cane was my return to River Forest Junior High for eighth grade. I knew I wouldn't be walking quickly from class to class like everyone else, and it seemed very possible that I might bump into someone in the hallway or run into some stationary object. I wanted to have the cane out just to remind others that I had a good reason for whatever clumsiness I displayed.

But the cane did more than that. As I made my way through the hallways going to class, I felt like Moses parting the Red Sea! People scrambled to get out of my way, just like my dad had noticed already. I've always wished I could have seen the expressions on their faces when they saw me. Were they simply recognizing that I was coming and casually getting out of my way, or did their faces show panic and foreboding that I was just about to crash into them?

I also soon noticed that the cane had the same effect on people walking near me on the street. One time I was walking in downtown Oak Park, and I could tell a mother and child were walking toward me. The mother must not have noticed me until they were about three feet away. I was just about to move a half step to the side to avoid bumping into them when she suddenly grabbed her small child and yanked him to the side!

Her reaction was so sudden and took her child so much by

surprise that I felt like apologizing to both of them. But then I realized that if I admitted I could see them coming, even if it was only at the last minute, that mom was going to feel pretty bad about jerking her child out of my way! So I said nothing and continued on my way. But the power of the white cane had finally gotten through to me in a big way.

Once I began to feel more comfortable using my collapsible white cane, I took it a bit for granted. I figured everyone in the world knew what a white cane was and why I was using one. But that wasn't entirely true. One day during the summer after eighth grade, I was walking through Keystone Field, the main park in River Forest. I had spent many, many hours in Keystone Field because that's also where I had played Little League for six summers on the park's three diamonds. My memories of those games were still very vivid. They had been some of the best times of my life.

But as I walked now, I knew I would not play baseball on any of those diamonds anytime soon. I couldn't even see the players well enough to watch the games anymore. If my optic nerves never healed (at this point I remained convinced that they might), baseball would never be a part of my life again— either playing or watching—and that was certainly not any kind of reality I wanted to face.

So I was feeling a bit melancholy as I made my way through the park. I moved slowly because I was not using my white cane; it was folded up and sticking out of my back pocket. After all, I was in familiar territory, and I was determined not to look like a "sad blind person" trying to find his way through the park. I was sure I could do this by myself with no need for the cane.

Well, I did get almost all the way across the park just fine. But as I neared the far side, a woman came right up to me and practically shouted, "I am sick and tired of you boys causing trouble around here!"

I was caught totally off guard. "I'm sorry, what are you talking about?" I asked respectfully. But her stern and annoyed temperament was undiminished.

"It's those fireworks you've been setting off!" she answered. "It's those firecrackers in your back pocket. They're dangerous to everyone around!"

I realized then that she thought my folded-up white cane was some kind of firecracker! My folks had taught all of us to always consider other adults as being in authority and speak to them with respect, but I have to admit, I was a little miffed about this encounter.

I reached into my back pocket and pulled out the cane and said, "It's not fireworks; it's my white cane. I'm legally blind!"

I emphasized the word *blind*, and it got just the reaction I was looking for.

The woman was speechless for a moment, but then said, "Oh, I see." She didn't apologize or add anything further; she just turned and walked away.

After this I filed a short "note to self:" Some adults don't feel comfortable, or think it necessary, to apologize to children—especially teenage boys. This also helped me realize that very few people recognize a collapsible white cane when they see it. So there was no reason for me to feel self-conscious about carrying one around.

Chapter 3:   Life as a Teenaged VIP

INTRODUCTION TO OPRF

My school environment got a lot more challenging as I made my way through the halls of Oak Park River Forest High School for ninth grade. OPRF had four floors and more than 120 classrooms. The door numbers were again on the top of the door jamb, but I had no prior knowledge of the layout to help me. And now there weren't just dozens of people walking next to and by me, there were hundreds. (There were more than 4200 students at OPRF in 1974.) I soon discovered that the more people around, the lonelier I felt.

In addition, my problems with failing shunts continued. Ultimately, the time I spent at the junior high and those first years of high school was just a side show, as I spent most of my time from 1969 to 1972 either at the hospital or recovering from surgery at home.

When I was at the hospital, my Mom woke up and took care of getting Dad, Pete, Karen, and JoAnne fed and off to work and school, as well as taking care of Mary Christine. Then, on many days she drove to downtown Chicago to be with me in the hospital. She stayed with me until early afternoon, when she would head home to help everyone else after school was over.

When he wasn't traveling for work, some evenings Dad came to the hospital, and he always stayed until visiting hours were over. My parents made sure I never felt cut off from my family during my hospital stays.

After every return from the hospital to put in a new shunt, which I'd done four times by the time I started ninth grade, everyone hoped the newest replacement would work. The surgery and technology being used was all pretty new, so there wasn't much history of past operations to reference. I made three trips to Illinois Masonic during my freshman year to change shunts. And because there were no tests to tell the doctors anything or indicate that something different might be more helpful, I just came in and had surgery to remove the old shunt and implant a new one. Then I rested in the hospital for a couple days before going home for several additional days of rest.

My freshman year ended up being two semesters of three weeks off and six weeks on. Dr. Pawl says now it was amazing that I didn't develop an infection from all the operations during eighth and ninth grade. Still, every operation could have been the one that finally worked, so once I started to recover, everyone focused on getting me back into the mainstream. This meant signing up for classes and working to get all my textbooks for the next semester taped.

Getting through eighth grade had shown me I was qualified and capable enough to get through classes, even with these surgeries and my failing eyesight. Pete continued to be there for me as we started high school, and the OPRF faculty proved themselves willing to adapt to the accommodations I needed.

LISTEN TO THE PROS (MOST OF THE TIME)

Al Ogden, Pete's and my dean for our four years at OPRF, entered my life in ninth grade and soon became an important presence. Mr. Ogden and I would have met regardless of my vision problem, as deans were assigned to students based on the spelling of their last name. However, Mr. Ogden and I had a unique relationship, unlike any other student and dean at the school, as my issues made me unlike any student the school had ever had.

As junior high was wrapping up for me, my parents must certainly have visited OPRF to scope out the dean I would be assigned to and discuss how feasible it was for me to attend the local high school and succeed there. In 1970, Illinois State Law dictated that high school students with visual disabilities be transported from their home each day to the "regional high school equipped for students with visual impairments." This would have meant a 40-minute cab ride back and forth to a high school 24 miles away from home every day. What made these schools "equipped" was that they had a resource teacher on staff who was qualified to work with students with visual impairments.

The fact that Pete would be attending school as well, although maybe not having every class with me, had to be a big factor in everyone deciding to let me give OPRF a try. But this meant I was bucking the system, and it took a lot of effort on my folks' part to get the new arrangement approved. Both my parents were graduates of OPRF, and they wanted me to remain a part of the community, not go away to another high school. They knew how nice it was to attend a neighborhood school, as it was less than a mile away from our house and even walkable during the spring and fall. And, in the back of their minds, they knew that being closer to home would be critical if the shunt were to fail during school. Luckily, all the remaining seizures and trips to Illinois Masonic occurred at night.

Knowing Mr. Ogden as I do today, I'm sure my situation represented a bit of a personal challenge to him. He was the kind of dean who did everything in his power for the best interest of the student, even if that meant going outside accepted standards or practices. He was very popular with both his students and their parents. I heard this from other classmates quite a bit. So, between my parents and Mr. Ogden, I had a mighty alliance of support to give OPRF a try.

I visited Mr. Ogden's office many, many times during my years at OPRF, but I distinctly remember one of my first trips there. The deans' offices were set up in clumps at the high school. When a student entered the office, he checked in with a receptionist and then took a seat until his dean was able to see him. While I was waiting, I couldn't help but overhear Mr. Ogden speaking to a student in his office, and he was not a happy camper! The girl had obviously been to his office with problems before, and she was there now because she had refused to behave the way Dean Ogden had told her she must. His words were forceful and no nonsense, but he did not cross over the line to a yell. Nonetheless, he seemed to be in such a foul mood that I considered getting up and coming back some other time. But I stayed. When it was my turn to go in, I sheepishly entered with some kind of salutation like, "I'm really sorry to bother you, Mr. Ogden, but..."

But his greeting to me was positive and upbeat! There was no sign that his difficult prior meeting was going to influence mine. Nevertheless, that early glimpse of him left an impression that caused me to always begin our meetings with an apology for taking up his time. This persisted until one day when I arrived and he abruptly stopped me from talking. In the closest voice to a shout that I ever heard from him, he said, "For Pete's sake, stop apologizing every time you come in here!"

Although I was tempted to say "I'm sorry for apologizing all the time," I don't think I did.

His statement had a profound impact on my self-perception. It made me realize my visual problem was not my fault, and that people might not always feel inconvenienced when dealing with me. In many cases, such as Mr. Ogden's, dealing with my vision problem was as much a part of their responsibilities as it was mine. This was a huge step! Although being legally blind was a bit more unique and off the beaten path of physical maladies, it wasn't any more special or difficult to deal with than a person with a mobility problem, or even learning disability. It was just different.

During my four years in high school, Mr. Ogden was my wise and benign counsel and benefactor. I am sure that he, behind the scenes, met with my teachers before the semester began and made sure they were willing and able to adapt their teaching to accommodate me—and this was no easy task. First of all, there was my Brailler: a ten-pound contraption I carried from class to class and took my notes with. As I did so, it made a *kachung, kachung* noise with each character I typed, and it ended each line with a bing! Then I would manually push the line-up button and return the point of the Braille writer to the beginning of the line. Being in a class with me meant enduring a constant chorus of *kachung, kachung, kachung, kachung, bing, zip, click!* I am deeply grateful to all my teachers and fellow students who put up with that. It comforts me to think that today's visually impaired students probably use talking laptops with ear plugs or some other technology that's less disruptive to those around them.

As I mentioned, from the first day I attended classes at OPRF, finding my classrooms and making my way through the crowded hallways of the school were huge challenges. Mr. Ogden helped me get my schedule of classes prior to the first day of school, and he got me access to the school so I could map out the best way to move from class to class in advance. Without this, trying to move through the hallways to my classrooms with 4000 other students would have been impossible in the few minutes allowed.

Instead, I went in to find my classrooms before the semester started, and then I would make a "treasure map" of sorts with directions to each room, like: take east stairs to third floor, center hall to third room on right. I would only need to use these directions for a couple of weeks, until I had the routes down. Then I'd start all over again the next semester.

Eventually, I found myself paying close attention to my own movements when I found myself in a new environment. I came to call this process "using mental breadcrumbs" when moving in an unfamiliar environment. I do it now instinctively when I enter someone's home, a restaurant, a hotel, or a movie theater. And I have two big priorities: I never forget where a bathroom is, and I remember steps! I never trip on the same step twice.

Patricia Burrows was another adult who made a huge difference during those first years of transition to my new reality. She was the the resource teacher at Proviso West High School in the early 1970s. Proviso was the high school I was supposed to attend as a visually impaired student, and I suspect that Mrs. Burrows is the person who eventually signed off on the decision to let me attend OPRF. She volunteered to come to OPRF for a couple hours twice a week to help me with anything I needed, rather than me traveling to her school five days a week.

Despite this, my memory is that my time with Mrs. Burrows did not start particularly well. She worked with me a great deal on improving my Braille-reading ability, and I tried to practice between our sessions, but it always seemed that other scholastic responsibilities took up my time.

At the end of my first semester of freshman year, my family took a long driving trip down to Florida. (Luckily, my shunt had been replaced a few weeks before we left, so we had good reason to believe that there would not be a shunt failure while we were out of town.) Before I left, I got a Braille book from Mrs. Burrows. It was titled *Animal Farm*. My dad did a lot of the driving at night, and I sat in the front passenger's seat and read my book. My dad looked over at me several times and tried to wake me up because he thought I had fallen asleep, or worse, was having a seizure. My chin was on my chest and my hands were on my book on my lap, but he could not see my hands moving as I read the book. I was hooked on the book, and my fascination with *Animal Farm* kept me wanting to read more of the story and inadvertently kept me practicing my Braille!

When I returned, Mrs. Burrows was amazed at how much my Braille reading had improved. For the next four years, she regularly stopped by my high school and assisted me in many ways. As she did so, I remember thinking that maybe my vision problem would not hold me back in life as much as I'd first thought. I know I was afraid that if I admitted to myself that I was now legally blind, I was accepting a designation that would pretty much institutionalize my life. I would be forced to accept that there were many, many things I would never be able to do, and I didn't want to do that.

SUPPORT MAKES THE DIFFERENCE

When classes began my freshman year, it had only been 18 months since the loss of my sight, and my movements were still tentative. Pete and I had most of our classes together freshman year, so we moved together from class to class, but we had fewer classes in common each year after that. I always had my white cane out between classes so other students would give me a wider berth when moving past, or at least not punch me if I bumped into them.

However, I was involved in an altercation my freshman year. I was in a hallway, walking to my next class without Pete when a fellow smacked into me from my left side. Before I could muster a humble apology, a second guy grabbed the first guy and threw him against the lockers.

"Hey! Watch where you're going," he yelled.

I immediately recognized the voice as Carl from my grade school. Carl was known to all as someone you didn't mess with, but I had always made it a point to be friendly to him. I never thought he felt any kind of friendship toward me, but now, here he was acting as my hallway bodyguard. He turned and motioned broadly for me to continue to my class.

"Hey, thanks!" I said, and proceeded on my way.

During high school, There were three friends with whom Pete and I did most things: Kevin Hanley, Dave Beeman, and Dick Mason. Kevin, Dave, and Dick all learned how to watch a movie from the fifth row of the theater while we were in high school together. Sitting that close enabled me to catch the major movements and theme of most movies, although there always were a handful of questions I had to ask like, "What did that subtitle just say?" or "Who was that guy who just spoke?" They were all great sports to make that accommodation for me.

But far and away the best example of someone going the extra mile for me was when Pete went with me to see *Das Boot*. The movie was the story of a German U-boat crew during the Second World War, and it was all in German, with English subtitles. Pete knew I wanted to see it badly, so we went, found some seats away from others, and he proceeded to read the whole movie for me! Ironically, the movie ended up being so successful in the United States that a dubbed English version came out a year or so later.

As far as keeping ourselves entertained, simply driving to someone else's house to see what they were doing was the regular routine. Interspersed throughout were sorties to downtown Chicago, about 10 miles away, where we would pick up pizza or, on a big night, attend a show at The Second City, Chicago's premier comedy club. And if we didn't want to drive far for food, there was always Peterson's Ice Cream Parlor in Oak Park, which was just three blocks from both my house and Dick's house. Because I could never help with the driving, I was always looking for ways to contribute to the evening out. After we discovered that my white cane regularly got us all the best seats in the house, as well as good service, everyone made sure I was the first of our group in the door when we went out.

by John H. Erickson

MY BEST NEW FRIEND

Though I was thankful for these long-standing friendships, I did, of course, make some new friends in high school as well. The first of several people who would become great friends of mine, and who I never would have met if not for my visual impairment, was Cindy Dillon. I met Cindy when I started my freshman year. Dean Ogden had realized that the conventional study halls students had during the school day would be of no help to me. Not only would I need lots of space for my Braille writer, magic markers, reams of scratch paper, and reel-to-reel tape player to listen to my taped textbooks, I would need privacy to listen to them, and I would often need an actual person to read to me handouts and other materials I could not get taped.

So Mr. Ogden coordinated most of my study halls each week to match up with Cindy's, and he commandeered a small storage closet for me to go to with Cindy during my study halls. I never did ask her if she was asked to volunteer for my reading job, or if she was able to use it as something on her college applications, perhaps as an extracurricular, public service activity. Quite frankly, I never cared why she was there—I was just glad she was.

When we first met, Cindy was a junior and on her way to becoming one of her class's valedictorians. Of much more interest to me, she was gorgeous! Not only was Cindy smart, she was nice, friendly, easy to talk to—and she was blond. She was an enormous help to me scholastically during my first two years of high school, especially freshman year when I was trying to get my feet on the ground in this new environment. She also had another significant influence on me: Although we never dated, she was the reason I found myself dating only blond women for the next ten years, and finally marrying one!

Cindy never called me John. Her name for me was Juanito. I was flattered by her use of such a friendly and familiar nickname, and it stuck for as long as we knew each other. My room, as I came to call it, was on the third floor of the high school, just off one of the major staircases. Its ten-by-eight-foot dimensions were just large enough to handle a table a little bigger than a card table and two chairs. In one corner, a six-inch pipe ran from the floor to the ceiling. Although I was initially assigned a locker like all other freshman, I never used it once I realized my room would do a better job of serving as my locker too. Within the first week of school, a self-standing coat hanger and very small end table found their way to my room.

But the nicest touch came during my second semester when Cindy bought me a poster: a view of a man entering a manhole, from inside the manhole. We borrowed scotch tape from one of the teachers and proceeded to affix the poster to the ceiling of my room. After that we could pretend we were working in the sewer. In later years I added one or two other posters to the walls of my room, but I never took down Cindy's poster, which I cherished.

I never decorated or put any kind of marking on the outside door of my room, as I relished its privacy and clandestine nature. There were more than a couple times that good friends asked me if they could borrow the key to my room to take a nap after some kind of long night before.

My sessions with Cindy were primarily business: reading handouts from teachers and reviewing my lessons and homework. But we always found a couple free minutes to talk about dances and things that were going on. Cindy shared just enough information about her social life for me to know she didn't sit around the house much at night and never missed a Prom or homecoming dance.

LAST RITES AT 16

During my sophomore year of high school, on February 2, 1972, I had another seizure at night and returned to Illinois Masonic Medical Center.

Many years later, my father told me Dr. Pawl had told him and my mother the very grim news that night that there was no sense in replacing the shunt anymore. It wasn't working, and the doctors didn't know why. There was nothing else they could do to make me better, so it would not be long before I passed away. Father O'Connor, a priest from St. Luke's, our church, and a close friend of my parents, came to the hospital and gave me the Sacrament of Last Rites.

I was now unconscious due to the seizure from the pressure on the brain. Because I wouldn't suffer no matter what happened now, Dr. Pawl asked my parents' permission to do one more exploratory operation. He wanted to try an experimental shunt procedure in the back of my neck. It had been tried on a few others, but discontinued as too risky for the potential benefit in every way. However, with no options remaining, my parents agreed.

"When [Dr. Pawl] opened you up, the pressure just poured out, and your vital signs started to come back," my dad told me years later. So during this operation, not only was the shunt that ran down the right side of my neck replaced, but a second shunt was inserted that ran down the back of my head. This second shunt was dangerously close to my spinal cord, and the risks of something going wrong were great, but there were no better ideas, Dr. Pawl eventually explained to me.

"After that procedure you came back pretty strong, and even though I think we all thought it would again be just temporary, we were glad to have whatever time with you the Good Lord intended you to have," my dad later told me.

"While all this was going on, and all the way through your recovery, you can imagine how many times your mother made the trip back and forth [to the hospital] while still managing to take care of and give as comfortable a home life as possible to your brother and sisters," he added. "[She made sure] their lives did not come to a standstill."

A TRUE VIP

Now my right eye was totally blind, and the vision in my left eye was like being surrounded by heavy fog. In the very center of that eye, the fog was so thick I could not see anything through it. The bottom left quadrant of that eye was where the fog was the thinnest. Although I was still unable to read any kind of printed type, I could see things like thick magic marker writing in 2-inch-high letters, or the contrast of a dark mountain against the sky many miles away.

During a subsequent visit to a new eye doctor, I asked just exactly what my visual acuity was. This was an eye doctor who specialized with "low vision" patients. Once I could not read any of the letters on the standard eye chart, my first eye doctor had no insights to offer. But the new doctor picked up the chart and brought it closer and closer until I could make out the largest of the letters. He noted how far away I was from the chart and did some calculations.

Very roughly, he estimated the visual acuity in the best

part of my left eye to be approximately 20/1000. I knew the definition of partially sighted was an acuity of 20/200 or worse, and the definition of legally blind was an acuity of less than 20/400. Because I had met other legally blind persons in the previous two years and saw what they could and couldn't do, and I knew pretty well where I was; I just wanted some numbers to explain it.

I actually felt better knowing my estimated acuity because it helped me to cut myself some slack when I got impatient or frustrated with my "visual inconvenience."

My eyesight remains like this today. But it hasn't gotten worse, and I've never had to go back for another operation.

REBUILDING TIME FOR BIG JOHN

The rest of my sophomore year at OPRF became the beginning of my "rebuilding era." All the efforts to catch up and stay on track with school began to build on each other, and my grades began to improve. Mr. Ogden even put me into a handful of honors and advanced placement classes, where one of my classmates was my brother Pete. These succeeded in restoring my confidence in my academic abilities.

Along with my self-perception, another of my rebuilding experiences at OPRF was improving my physical condition. Since freshman year, I had been assigned to the pool for physical education. All students were required to take at least one semester of swimming, but I'd been stuck there since high school began. However, now I began attending the remedial training class, where mostly injured athletes worked with progressive resistance machines. I really enjoyed this opportunity to add some weight by adding muscle—as I knew so well, thanks to my junior high gym teacher.

By my sophomore year, my relationship with Mr. Ogden had matured quite a bit. He was a facilitator for me—lending advice and influence to my challenges at the high school. I don't think I'd been a helpless, clueless freshman either, as he regularly addressed me as "Big John, Big John, Big Bad John." This was, of course, right from the Jimmy Dean song of that time, but that wasn't the kind of music my friends and I were listening to, so the full cleverness of the greeting was not completely appreciated until many years later when all songs of that time period became favorites of mine!

Also during sophomore year, Dad and I experienced the only unsuccessful accommodation attempt for me that I can ever remember. It was clear to everyone that the onset of driver's ed for Pete and all my friends had made me slightly depressed. It was one more item to add to the "can't do" list, and it was also a blow to my own self evaluation. More specifically, I saw myself as a less desirable date since I couldn't drive—if and when an opportunity to go out on a date ever came up.

So Dad had an idea that I could be in charge of backing out our family car from the garage and bringing it to the front of the house. He and I had some dry-run lessons in the car regarding the gearshift, brake, and gas pedal. I learned to start the car, put it in gear, and by cracking the driver's side door, I could see and follow the edge of the driveway out to the front of the house. The whole time, someone would watch to make sure no person or pets got in harm's way.

After a couple successful runs, our friend Kevin came to the house one night to go to the movies. While Pete made sure no one was in the way, I started to back the car out. I was beside the house when Kevin came running. He shouted that I should stop, put the car in park, and get out so he could drive.

I put the car in what I thought was park and started to climb out. But the car was in reverse, and as I tried to exit, it started rolling backward! Kevin couldn't reach the brake because I was in the way, so the car gently swerved and rolled right into our house with the worst scraping noise! That ended my driving for a long time.

By this time, I had been using my closed circuit television camera (CCTV) at home for three years. The CCTV had become my primary electronic tool to aid with reading. It sat on a tabletop and had a movable tray about 15 inches square. Mounted above the tray was a television camera that pointed straight down and took a picture of an area about one inch big, then blew it up onto a 15-inch television monitor that sat next to the tray. This enlarged printed type enough for me to read it, so it was great for reading typed letters, soup can instructions, and prescription bottles.

For three years, I had not built any model tanks or planes because of my sight. I could no longer see the parts or read the assembly instructions. I had pretty much concluded that I would never build another model. But I decided one day I would buy a simple model and try to use the CCTV to build it. To my delight, it worked just fine.

It was, of course, a very long and tedious process since I had to read the instructions, identify which parts of the model I needed, find them on the racks of model parts, then glue them together—all with the help of the CCTV. I repeated these steps over and over and over again until the model was complete. But the inconvenience didn't matter. I was so excited to discover a way to recapture a part of my life

I'd thought was lost forever. Today, building models is my favorite at-home pastime.

EARNING SOME SLACK

In December of 1972, another incident occurred that revealed the power of the white cane. About six months after we turned 16, Pete and I found ourselves at the Selective Service Office. Several weeks earlier, we'd gotten a letter notifying us that we were six months late in registering for the draft. We immediately made plans to visit the office and fully expected to be reprimanded for failing to register.

When we entered the office of the Selective Service rep, I had my cane out, and I could tell the guy did a double-take at the two of us. We sat down, and he asked, "Why are you guys six months late in registering with us?"

There had been my trip to the hospital about ten months before, but that now seemed long, long ago, and not relevant to answering his question. But while I was racking my brain for something else to tell him, Pete said, "Well, my brother's blind."

I remember thinking, *Well, yeah, duh! I think he already knows that, Pete. And what does my eyesight have to do with us being so late coming here?*

But the guy looked at us and said, "Oh, okay."

And that was it! We were excused. As Pete and I walked out of the office, I commended Pete for his quick thinking. We were both amazed it had worked.

My "note to self" about this incident was that most people will give a lot of latitude to someone with a visual disability, probably because they think much like I did when I first lost my sight. They can't imagine how they would live a normal life if they couldn't see everything, and they would certainly want others to cut them some slack!

It was also during my sophomore year at OPRF that a unique opportunity came up. The student who'd been elected our sophomore class president moved away early in the year, so there was a special election to elect a new president. This was just two months after I returned to school after my operation. I had not taken any interest in any such elected office since I first loss my sight because filling such a role seemed to me to be something I could never do. I happened to ask Mr. Ogden what kind of responsibilities there were for such an elected position, and he detected that I had some interest. He assured me that I had all the ability needed to do such a job, so I ran for the office.

It was a lucky thing for me that River Forest Junior High was the largest school that fed into OPRF. Most students were still just beginning to make friends with students from the Oak Park junior highs, so I think more students recognized my name and voted for me because of that. It was just like those elections for judges when you know nothing about the actual people, so you vote for the only familiar name you see! And perhaps my operations during freshman year gave me the sympathy vote too. But like any true politician would say: You do whatever it takes to get the votes. It doesn't matter how!

Mr. Ogden showed me that my life was not going to stop just because I was legally blind. This is what my parents had also tried so hard to show me, but I needed an outside authority to confirm it. Mr. Ogden and Mrs. Burrows always acted as though my future was no different than that of most students at OPRF: I would graduate and go on to complete college too.

My four years with them were the time I needed to build my confidence in what I could do, rather than focus on the things I'd had to leave behind. With the help of my parents, Mr. Ogden, Mrs. Burrows, Pete, and my friends, I started to believe that just maybe, my life could be not that much different than anyone else's. I would just need a little help from time to time.

A HUGE STEP BACK INTO SPORTS

Still, it was impossible to avoid recognizing that participating in sports with Pete and my friends was a thing of the past. I could still follow sports and attend games with friends, but I would no longer be playing them myself. During high school, I always went with Pete and my friends to any of the Cubs games, Sox games, and even Blackhawk games in Chicago they were going to. I learned to take a transistor radio with me so I could listen to the play-by-play and understand what I couldn't see happening in front of me.

I'd also learned that working outside the system was sometimes best. Before my eyesight challenges began, I was content to accept all the rules and parameters put upon me. After all, I believed the rules had been made by the experts, and for a reason, even if I didn't know what that reason was. I'd found that working within the rules pleased most people in authority, and this was the best way to get ahead. But now, after my experiences early in high school, I was starting to understand that sometimes new ideas and new ways of doing things could be better than the current, sanctioned way. This was a big step for me. After all, I would not even be attending OPRF with Pete and my friends if my folks had simply followed policy and let me be taken to the regional high school for visually impaired students!

One day during my sophomore year, Mrs. Burrows asked me if I was interested in downhill skiing. She told me there was a new organization called the American Blind Skiing Foundation in Chicago (ABSF), and they were looking for people to join. I had never done downhill skiing before I lost my sight, so I told her I probably wasn't qualified. But she said that didn't matter. She thought they would teach me. So I decided to give it a try.

Apart from Young Life, a Christian social organization, I was not involved in any other activities outside of school at that time. Keeping up with classes took up a huge part of my day. Because I had to listen to my books on tape, rather than reading them, I used to figure that if a teacher said she was assigning an hour of reading homework, I could count on it taking me one and a half to two hours to complete.

But that night I went home and told my parents about ABSF. A little bit to my surprise, my dad seemed really excited to hear about the program. I realize now that he was very involved with finding answers to the limitations I faced every day. He was always looking for opportunities for me to try new things. He'd made sure I could still sail at the cottage, he'd tried his best to get me behind the wheel of a car, and now he was eagerly supportive of skiing. He never showed me any of the worry or despair he might have been feeling- knowing that there would not be another saving operation if the shunt failed again. and I know his positive attitude was contagious to me. Hey, if my dad wasn't worried or depressed about this whole debacle, I wasn't going to be either! I trusted him, and if he thought skiing was worth trying, I was on board.

However, that's not to say I didn't have down days too.

There were nights when I was very frustrated that my taped reading took so long to get through. And because I'd just learned to read Braille a couple years before, it took lots of extra time to review my notes. But there was no giving up, because I didn't want to slip a year behind Pete. I wanted us both to leave home for college at the same time.

Anyway, within just a couple of weeks, my dad and I drove about an hour away to a small ski resort called Four Lakes to the west of Chicago. As we got closer, I got more and more excited to give the whole thing a try. I really got enthused when we went to the ski rental area and fitted ourselves with all the equipment. *This is great— it's like being a gladiator,* I thought.

The program organizers had gathered a group of professional ski instructors to serve as teachers and one-on-one guides for the blind skiers, but because so many blind skiers had showed up—more than anyone seemed to have expected—about half of us had to sit out either the morning or the afternoon while the limited number of instructors worked with the rest of skiers. I was one of the lucky skiers to go out first, and I loved it!

Every skier worked with his or her own guide. Both the skier and guide wore bright orange bibs that said either Blind Skier or Guide so other skiers wouldn't assume we could see and avoid them, if necessary. Instead they would give us plenty of space. Then, depending on how much sight the skier actually had, the guide would either lead her down the hill or ski behind him and give vocal commands all the way down.

When you're teaching someone with a visual impairment, you can't just say, "Watch me and do it this way." As I like to put it, you have to teach from the inside out. For skiing, this means not saying "bend your knee like this," but "bend your knee so you feel your shin against the tongue of your boot," or "keep your arms bent while skiing, as if you're carrying a tray down the slope." This definitely makes the teaching a bit more challenging.

I much preferred that the guide ski in front of me and I follow down the hill. Even though all the skiing that first day took place on either flat ground or the bunny hill, the feeling of moving while making small adjustments to change speed and direction felt like finally being part of driver's education. Now, with ABSF, I was doing driving of my own!

Anyway, ABSF offered ski opportunities almost every weekend, January through mid March, but they never got any more instructors, so there was always the half-day of waiting for some of the skiers. After Dad and I participated in the program for several weeks, some of the ABSF leaders took note of how well we moved together to and from the ski area and within the ski lodge. Since the first days of my sight loss, we had become accustomed to walking together, and we now moved very quickly. The ABSF leaders asked my dad if he would consider trying to be a ski guide for me.

Now, my dad had not skied a day in his life. However, we also were not talking about skiing at high speeds in those early days. So, he slapped on a pair of skis and a bright orange guide bib, and we took off. At this time, my dad was about 46 years old. Only when I reached the age of 46 myself did the true scope of my dad's courage, love, and dedication to me really sink in!

The leaders of ABSF took note of our progress too. During my second or third season of skiing, the small number of professional ski instructors was gradually replaced by a full compliment of solid, intermediate-skiing volunteers. I don't think any skier in the program would dispute that the key to a safe, fun, successful day of skiing is more dependent on the trust and communication between skier and guide than the skiing proficiency of the guide.

Skiing had an enormous effect on my self-confidence. It also signaled my re-entry into sports. Later in high school, and again in both college and graduate school, I joined friends and went skiing with them, using all the techniques and procedures ABSF had taught me. Many times a friend would remark, "Wow, you can ski?" And each time I answered, "Yeah!" I believed it more and more myself. I suddenly realized I'd written off skiing as something I could never do because of my sight. Now, since I could ski, I began to realize there were probably lots of other things I could do too.

BAD EYESIGHT DOESN'T MAKE YOU A BAD DATE

When my junior year of high school came around, I was finally starting to feel pretty good about myself again. But the one part of life I felt I was still missing out on was dating.

Some of my friends had girlfriends. In most cases they'd spotted them from afar, called them on the phone, and finally went out on a date with them using their family's car. I couldn't figure out the logistics of even just finding someone I'd like to go out with. I couldn't see that far. And how would I make the whole date work if I couldn't drive?

I briefly considered asking Pete or one of my friends to help me set up a double date, but that made me feel like some pitiful loser.

There also was a new issue that bothered me when I thought about it. My right eye had now been totally blind for a whole year, and the muscles that had held it in line with the left eye were no longer working. So my right eye had become a "lazy eye" and now looked off to the right, rather than moving with the left. Just to myself, I called it my "evil eye."

I couldn't see myself in the mirror well enough each morning to be reminded of the problem, but that lazy eye caused me to flinch whenever I looked at a picture of myself under my CCTV enlarger. I did not like it one bit, but there was nothing I could do about it. I wondered if it would prevent girls from wanting to go out with me, but I didn't stop trying.

I wanted to go out with someone, and I wanted to do this myself. Junior Prom finally gave me the opportunity! All during junior year, I had an American history class where a really cute girl sat behind me. It was one of the few classes in high school that had assigned seating, and with the same person sitting next to me day after day, I was able to memorize who my classmates were.

Her name was Karen, and she was sweet, smart, and seemed to enjoy my jokes. Also, needless to say, Karen was a blond. Junior Prom seemed like an event many people would be going to, even if they weren't in a serious relationship. So I got Karen's number and thought out a whole script of not only how I would ask her to the Prom, but also what I would say if she turned me down. Not having something to say at that point would be incredibly awkward, so I wanted that well covered.

Well, I made the phone call, but an awkward moment appeared anyway: I had nothing to say after she said yes to my invitation. All I could come up with at the spur of the moment was, "Uh, well, I guess I'll be calling you back later, right? Thanks a lot."

Karen and I double dated to the Prom with my good friend Dick Mason and his girlfriend. The best part of the night was when I boldly asked if Karen wanted to go out again sometime, and she said yes to that question too.

Karen showed me that not being able to drive was no reason not to ask someone out. What I found so enjoyable about dating Karen was being a part of her life, and having her be a part of mine. She lived about nine blocks away, and I simply walked over to her house most of the time. That mobility training with my white cane was now paying off in spades! I could make my own plans and go to Karen's anytime I wanted. I didn't have to wait around helplessly until someone could give me a ride. I was actually less impaired when I used the cane. Dad had been right all along!

UNEXPECTED UPGRADE

It was also during junior year that I got an unexpected upgrade to my at-school study quarters. I came in one Monday morning and found a note on the door of my room telling me to come to Mr. Ogden's office. I went there immediately, and he told me my room had been moved to the fourth floor. When I saw the new room, I was amazed. It was four times the size of my old room and even had a skylight!

It seems the Oak Park Fire Department had done their standard inspection of the high school over the weekend, and when they came to my room they'd asked why a broom closet was furnished. When they were told a blind student studied there, they didn't like it at all. So, thanks to them, I enjoyed palatial accommodations for the rest of my high school career.

Cindy, my first faithful reader and friend, had graduated at the end of my sophomore year. She went on to Wesleyan College and then to graduate school, but Mr. Ogden arranged for several other volunteer readers to assist me during my junior and senior years. However, I became much more productive on my own as my high school career progressed, so I needed less one-on-one reading help after Cindy's graduation. Therefore I was never as close with my other reading helpers as I had been with her.

HIGH SCHOOL FINALE

During my senior year of high school, everything finally seemed to come together. It had now been almost two years since my shunt last failed, and I slowly felt a growing sense of confidence in my physical health. I began to believe that maybe my regular trips to the hospital were finally over! Pete was now able to use the family car to drive us to high school in the morning, so our tandem bike got a rest.

Karen and I continued dating all year long. We'd sometimes rendezvous in my room during the school day, and we had lunch together most of the time. Her house was the same direction from the high school as mine, so we'd also walk home most of the way together.

Karen's friendship was a big help, but a nagging doubt about whether anyone would ever really find me attractive and worth being in a relationship with would be with me for many years to come. However, when college came and Karen and I went different ways, the time we'd enjoyed together made it easier for both of us to realize there were a lot of other people in the world we wanted to meet—and who might want to meet us too.

I saw Karen at our ten-year Oak Park-River Forest High School reunion. She made a point to find me and show me a picture of her baby boy. Though I couldn't see the details of the baby's face, I could tell how happy and proud she was. It was great to know she went on to a good life too.

One of my last classes at OPRF was creative writing with Mr. McGintey. We learned to write short stories, poems, and limericks. I enjoyed the class and used it to hone my skill at writing alternate funny lyrics to popular songs, just like my favorite section of *Mad* magazine. But my best memory of Mr. McGintey's class is the personal poem he wrote for each of us at the end of the semester. For me, Mr. McGintey recorded his note on a cassette tape. I remember that he concluded by explaining that the origin of the word *goodbye* is the phrase "God be with you." And if that were the case, he told me he was very pleased to say "Goodbye, John" at the end of this class.

Chapter 4:   The College Life

HERE COME THE IRISH!

When Pete and I began thinking about college, we initially agreed that it was probably a good idea if we went our separate ways and got some experience living with someone else. However, the tools and technology I had in the early 1970s were meager compared to what high school kids have today to help them research colleges. I was very ambivalent about where I would go. I knew I wanted a coed campus, because that's what I'd gotten used to at OPRF, and I wanted to make meeting girls as easy as possible! And I did not see any advantage to going to a school that was a lot bigger than OPRF, because it would pose additional challenges in getting around and finding the places I had to be.

Lucky for me, Pete had a very good idea of where he wanted to go: The University of Notre Dame in South Bend, Indiana. Pete always had been good at athletics, and he had once gone to a Notre Dame football game. He still remembered the spirit and enthusiasm for sports he'd witnessed there, and he wanted to go to a college where he could experience more of the same. At that time, 1973, there was no place better to do that than the University of Notre Dame.

Also, our maternal grandfather, Joe Carroll, had been quite the Notre Dame subway alum (someone who never attended the school, but carries a profound love for it anyway), and Pete had caught much of Grampa Joe's enthusiasm for the school.

So, early in our college search process, Pete announced he was going to take a "college day" off from high school and visit Notre Dame. Well, I'd never been to Notre Dame, and I figured visiting any kind of college campus would be helpful in making my own college selection, even if I was certain a big school like Notre Dame would never work for me. And besides, if Pete was going to get a day off of school, I was going to take a day off too! (This was part of the competitive twin mentality I had grown into over the past 17 years.)

When we visited Notre Dame, I was shocked to discover that there were only 6,000 undergraduate students there, not the tens of thousands that I had thought. This didn't seem like many more than the 4,000 students at OPRF, and at Notre Dame they were all spread out over a large campus, not crammed into a single building.

My mind began to turn. Notre Dame was also just two and a half hours away from home—far enough that I would not be tempted to run home during a crisis, but close enough to make holiday travel pretty easy. So my feelings about attending Notre Dame changed pretty quickly. However, Pete and I did agree that we'd stick with our agreement that we would not live together, even if we both got accepted.

During that first visit to Notre Dame, Pete, my dad, and I met with some people from the admissions office. At one point, my dad asked one of the admission counselors how realistic it was to think Pete and I could get into the university.

by John H. Erickson

After all, we were both B+ students, not straight A. The counselor said Pete and I had a chance because although Notre Dame could admit all straight A students if it wanted, Father Hesburgh, the president of the university, wanted a broad array of students at the school.

We were all relieved to hear that, so Pete and I sent in our applications and kept our fingers crossed!

In the fall of 1973, the beginning of our senior year at OPRF, Notre Dame won the college football national championship and we were all the more excited at the possibility of going to college there. But now we wondered if demand for the university would be greater, and our chances of getting in would be slimmer. So when we heard in the spring of 1974 that we both had indeed been accepted by Notre Dame, we were ecstatic!

Pete knew from the very beginning that he was going to be an architecture major at Notre Dame, or an "archie," as they were called. And he quickly decided he wanted to have the traditional experience, so he chose Morrissey Hall as his dorm. It was very close to the "archie building" where architecture students studied and took their classes. I, on the other hand, always felt that Morrissey, like many of the other traditional dorms, was a bit spartan. (During the winter months, the only way to regulate the temperature in any particular room was to adjust how much your one outside window was cracked open. The older dorms did not have air conditioning either.

I made my dorm choice during one of my subsequent visits to Notre Dame during the summer after my senior year of high school. One of the two newer, high-rise dorms, Flanner, was very different from the others. It was eleven stories high, had elevators for students to use, and most importantly, it was air conditioned! The decision was a lay-up: I was going to live in Flanner.

SETTLING IN

When the fall came, Pete and I packed up the car and drove with my parents to Notre Dame. We were greeted by students who offered to help us unpack and move in. At Flanner Hall, one of the students who offered his help was Ross Browner, a Notre Dame football player on his way to greatness in both his college and professional football career! I am about 5 feet, 8 inches tall, and I remember several times being on the elevator with Ross and other ND football players. I pretty much looked at their belt buckles or stomachs when I glanced over at them.

My new roommate was a nice guy, and we got along just fine, but he wasn't very adventurous. He knew what his major was going to be (I did not), and he knew what he was going to do in his free time (I did not). I wanted to go wandering around to meet people and check out places, but he did not. I realized I would have to depend on Pete or someone else to help me meet others and fully discover what Notre Dame and college life had to offer.

But, my immediate need was to get my arms around the demands of my classes and professors, and this did not go well at first. Unlike OPRF, there was no Mr. Ogden to help me plan classes, brief professors about me, or set up volunteer readers to handle the overflow of reading materials beyond the books I had already gotten recorded. There was no Department of Student Services at Notre Dame back then.

During my first week of classes, I had chemistry, which had been recommended for me, despite my reservations. The class met in a large auditorium. I took notes with my Brailler, which made its usual *kachung, kachung, bing, click, zip* noises. After class, the professor came to me and said my machine was disrupting the students around me, and I would have to find another way to take notes. So I tried to switch from taking Braille notes to writing them with a magic marker. This wasn't easy, but I did it for a whole semester. And then it dawned on me: this was ridiculous! So I did not take a second semester of chemistry, but switched to biology instead—something I would have thought unconscionable just six months earlier.

That ended up being the most significant *A-ha!* moment of my college career. I realized no one was going to tell me the answers to all my questions because there was no one who knew what I wanted and what I was capable of better than me! If I wanted the profs in my new classes to know about my Brailler, I had to tell them. If I needed readers to help with extra homework, I had to find them. It was time to start being the captain of my own ship because no one could plot a better course for my life than me.

I decided I would advertise for readers and pay them for their time. I wanted our relationship to have the importance of a business arrangement, not a volunteer opportunity. I discovered very quickly that the reading arrangements I made with female students worked out a lot better than the ones with male students. (Only then did I see Mr. Ogden's wisdom in setting up all female readers for me in high school.)

I think back on my whole adjustment to college as a tough love experience. It didn't mean Notre Dame cared for me any less than OPRF had; it just meant taking care of these things myself was something I'd have to do for the rest of my life, and the time had come to start doing so now!

A NEW FRIEND

One day during those first several weeks of college, I had just left Flanner and was making my way to class with my Brailler, folder of blank paper, and magic markers in one hand and my white cane in the other. Someone who looked like an upperclassman came up and asked me how things were going. For some reason, I didn't answer in my usual "just fine" way, but said something like, "Ha! Not so well. How about you?"

He seemed very interested in my reply and proceeded to ask me a lot of questions about my white cane, my Brailler, and my eyesight in general. By the end of our short walk together, he had offered to help me read anything I needed help with, and I discovered he not only lived on my floor in Flanner but was not an upperclassman, like I'd suspected, but a lowly freshman just like myself.

This was the first time I met Joe Camarda, and he was already on his way to becoming not only my roommate for the next three years, but my best friend at Notre Dame.

Years later, Joe said one of the luckiest moments in his life came a short time after this when he and I, as well as my dad, had a bit of a showdown over whether or not Joe would be paid for the reading he wanted to do for me. "The day I said, 'I do it for free or I don't do it' was a good day because that was the first bond of my most important college relationship," Joe said. "I often think about that."

Joe was not only friendly and outgoing, he was adventurous and just the kind of guy I wanted to hang out and experience college with. He even ended up being my unofficial college career counselor! Near the end of our freshman year, Joe asked me what I was going to declare as my major. Trying to be pragmatic and realistic, I said I had only heard of visually impaired people being teachers or lawyers, so I thought I was going to stay in General Program as my major. "What? Are you nuts?!" Joe exclaimed. "Business is where all the jobs are, and that's where there's money to be made!"

I thought about it for about two seconds and then agreed, "Yeah, I'll do business!"

It turned out to have been the perfect choice. After getting a taste of accounting, marketing, management, and finance, I was drawn to finance. I remembered back about ten years earlier when I had taken my little passbook into the bank to have the interest compounded. When the teller handed me the passbook back, I had received $1.86 in interest for doing absolutely nothing! At that time, Pete and I were doing chores around the house like cutting the grass and shoveling the sidewalk for a weekly allowance of 50 cents. And now the bank was going to give me three times that amount for doing nothing but letting them hold my money? I was all over that! I became a saver for the rest of my life. Majoring in finance would teach me how to do that even better, as well as eventually find my way to a job where I would tell others how to save and invest their money.

Joe and I became roommates sophomore year. Pete stayed in Morrissey Hall, but all three of us hung out together and explored the things Notre Dame and college life had to offer. For junior year, Pete and all his fellow archie classmates moved to the Notre Dame Architecture Program in Rome, Italy, for their classes, and Joe and I stayed on the Notre Dame campus as roommates.

As a side note, at Christmastime that year, my parents let me take another huge step in my quest for self-confidence and independence. I boarded a jetliner and flew to Rome to spend Christmas break with Pete and his archie friends. Just a few hours after I landed in Rome, a bunch of us boarded a train to Munich and were off for a two-week, six-country adventure around Europe.

I remember wondering what sort of reaction my white cane and I would receive from people in Europe, and I was surprised that many of them did not seem familiar with the idea of a visually impaired person traveling on his own. But I had a wonderful time, and after the adventure returned to Notre Dame for the rest of my junior year.

When I returned to campus that second semester, Joe had a surprise for me. He read a lot of books for pleasure, and he'd read one over the break he knew I would like. So before he came back to Notre Dame, he sat down and recorded the whole thing on cassette tapes. The book was *Marathon Man*, and it will always be my most favorite recorded book because the voice of the reader is my best friend.

"You were always kind and thoughtful—full of substance if a little light on self confidence," says Joe of me in college. "I never was too thoughtful and had no substance, but I had way, way, way, too much self confidence. We were a very good Punch and Judy, and we made each other better."

It's clear to me now that Joe engaged me in that first conversation because he was curious about the guy he saw walking with a white cane and Braille writing machine. I'm sure I would have come to know who Joe Camarda was during my four years at Notre Dame, but we would not have been drawn so closely together so early if not for my blindness.

by John H. Erickson

FINDING SOME PEACE

My time at Notre Dame went by quickly. There were classes during the day, and then there was reading and homework at night. Listening to all my books on tape, or having my readers read them to me, took at least an extra couple of hours a night. This extra demand on my time seriously cut into what was available for drinking and carousing, but that probably was not a bad thing in retrospect!

Most of my friends in high school had known me before my vision loss, so they knew I was really just a regular guy. But like Joe, all the friends I would make for the rest of my life would know me only with my visual impairment. I suspected that the first thing people saw about me now was my blindness, and most weren't quite sure what to say or do about it. Having the white cane was a lot like being in a wheelchair—I wished I didn't need it, but it absolutely had to be there for some situations! Just as with my professors, I had to be the one to show and tell the new friends in my life what I wanted them to know about me. This is why my life has become more adventurous since my sight loss, not less!

Although I had come a long way in understanding the usefulness of my white cane, when I began college I'd still tried to use it only in the most necessary circumstances, such as crossing a street by myself, as I had done since eighth grade. In most social settings—going out to the bars or hitting a party on campus—I folded it up as quickly as I could and put it out of sight.

However, as my general level of confidence grew, I found myself in more and more unfamiliar places. Eventually my white cane became an indispensable tool for my own independence. At some point along the way, I realized that being visually impaired was like being four feet tall: I might not like it, but the sooner I accepted it, the sooner I could get on with living my life, rather than using all my energy moaning about this or that.

I do finally remember driving somewhere in the car with my dad during college and saying to him, "You know, if my eyesight never ever gets better again, I'm going to be okay." I had mentally reviewed the events of the previous seven years, since that very first trip to the hospital, and realized all I'd accomplished. I had gotten through all the operations, I had gone back to class and graduated high school, and now I was a student at The University of Notre Dame. I felt confident I would be able to get through that too.

I did not have grand expectations about landing a great job, or finding the love of my life and living happily ever after, but I knew I could find some kind of work and most likely support myself as an adult. I was reasonably confident I wasn't going to be homeless or starve. After all, I had already been able to find several different jobs over the years—at the River Forest Park District, at a restaurant called The Shingle Shack, and I'd done hours and hours of stuffing envelopes and preparing mailings for Hall-Erickson, Inc., the family business. I was not afraid to work, and that was all I needed to move on to another day.

In 1978 I graduated from Notre Dame with a bachelor's degree in business administration. In addition to that diploma, Notre Dame is also the origin of one of my most favorite bits of wisdom. Lou Holtz was Notre Dame's head football coach several years after Pete and I graduated. He retired from coaching in 1996, and I did something I have never done before or since: I wrote him a letter to wish him well in whatever he did next. To my utter amazement, he wrote me a short note back that said, "I don't know what the future holds, but I know who holds the future."

ALWAYS HAVE A BACK-UP PLAN

During the second semester of my senior year at Notre Dame, the spring of 1974, I began interviewing for jobs with any company that visited Notre Dame looking for graduates in the finance industry.

After doing some interviews, I talked with Joe and other classmates graduating from the business school, and I realized many of them were going into the interviews with a very different approach than I was.

Other students were doing a little research about the companies in advance, and then going into those interviews with a very positive, ambitious attitude, as if the job was exactly what they had been looking for their whole life! I really did not have a specific career in mind—How could I? I had never worked at a bank or insurance company or any kind of company in the finance industry, so it seemed dishonest to tell an interviewer that the job they had available was just what I wanted.

Sure, I wanted a job, but *any* job, and I would work extremely hard for anyone who hired me. However, I thought the interviewer was probably in a better position to evaluate whether I was a good fit for their position than I was.

So I also began thinking about a back-up plan. There was always a chance that none of my interviews would get me a job, and then what would I do? Of course, I could go home and continue interviewing for jobs, but I would not have any of the resources available there that I had here at Notre Dame. I wondered if my limited eyesight was proving to be a negative factor to potential employers. None of them mentioned it in any way, but if I wasn't able to get any job offers, despite a B+ grade point average and many interviews with a variety of companies, I had to consider that, right? I wanted a contingency plan.

My Notre Dame classes were over now, so I couldn't take anything new to improve my resume, nor could I change my grades in the classes I'd already taken. But what if I went on and got another degree? Would this offset any possible negative forces I was fighting due to my impaired vision? Maybe it would. So I applied to a couple different schools in the Midwest to get an MBA, even as I continued with the job interviews.

When time for graduation came at Notre Dame, I did not have any job offers, but I had been accepted into the Northwestern Graduate School of Management's MBA program in Chicago. So I made the decision to go there.

Chapter 5:   Life After College

OFF TO GRAD SCHOOL

In May 1978, when Notre Dame graduation and all the festivities were over in South Bend, Pete and I packed up our stuff at the apartment we'd lived in our senior year and said our goodbyes to Joe and all our other friends. Pete put some things in storage at Notre Dame since he would be coming back in the fall for the fifth year of his 5-year architecture degree, but I had to bring everything home in the car since my four years at Notre Dame were over.

I would be starting at Northwestern Graduate School of Management for my MBA in about three weeks. Northwestern had a unique MBA program that allowed you to receive your master's degree in just four quarters, but this also meant I had to start the program just weeks after graduating from Notre Dame.

When Pete and I arrived back in River Forest, there were some things I didn't even take out of the car, just so I did not have to pack them up again in a couple weeks. And those few weeks passed in a blink of an eye. Before I knew it, Pete had started his summer job at my dad's trade show and convention management company, Hall-Erickson Inc., and I left for Evanston to attend Northwestern.

I had decided to take a room in Engelhard Hall, the graduate school dorm on campus, for at least the first semester. Engelhard was an easy three-block walk to campus, straight down Davis Street. It was also just a half-block walk to the el train going from Evanston to Chicago. That el would also take me to downtown Evanston for shopping and restaurants. And if necessary, I could take the el to Chicago and then transfer to another el to get home to River Forest. I didn't see myself going home for any reason all semester, but I felt a little less anxious knowing I could get there totally on my own, if needed.

Because I was totally on my own now. Pete wouldn't be anywhere close by to lend a hand, like he had always been before. I'd known this time would come, inevitably, and now it was here. I decided this semester would be like the first semester of my junior year at Notre Dame, when Pete went off to Rome for his architecture studies. I would miss him a ton, sure, but I would hopefully see him when the semester at Northwestern was over, and at Thanksgiving for sure.

But there was a big difference now: I was in a brand new place, in unfamiliar surroundings, and I didn't know anyone! Yet there wasn't another option. This is what I had to do. I remember thinking the odds that I would find another Joe Camarda to hang with were slim to none, and likely the classes would be harder and my grades lower, so fun was probably going to be harder to find.

But it was only for one year. I could get through that. Right?

There were about 70 students in the program, and classes were intense and moved quickly. My roommate there was

by John H. Erickson

Dave Gimbert, or Boots as we came to call him. He was fun and adventurous and just what I was looking for!

Dave was very easygoing on the outside, but he wanted to be where the action was. He was quick to make friends with the other four-quarter students, and he was always asking where people were going and what they were doing.

Many of us in the four-quarter program had come right from undergraduate school, so being at Northwestern was sort of a second senior year for lots of us. My classmates were some of the most high-powered and intelligent people I have ever known, and I was surprised to find that practically all of them were also some of the nicest and friendliest people I have ever known.

TRYING NEW THINGS UNCOVERS NEW TALENTS

Part of me wanted to make up for lost time and have all the fun I should have had at Notre Dame. Because we were just about the only people on the Northwestern campus during that first summer quarter, our class did almost everything together—including having fun at night and on the weekends.

During one of our parties that first summer, I found myself dancing with the most beautiful girl I had ever met. Her name was Carol. How did I know she was beautiful? Well, she was fun and exciting, and her long hair was blond, of course. She was the perfect height: just a little shorter than me. Her face may have been a blur, especially that first night, but she was gorgeous to me. And for anyone, whether your vision is 20/20 or not, that's what matters.

In college I'd realized that our society (and maybe guys in particular) can get hung up on meaningless physical imperfections. One time, way back in high school, some guys had corrected me after I'd said a girl was cute. They said she had a "complexion problem." I'd thought to myself that it might not be so bad if everyone's eyesight was like mine. We'd all be less judgmental about petty appearances. Although, for the record, no one ever corrected me about Carol.

I had not really done any dating during my undergraduate years at Notre Dame, primarily because keeping up with classes was so challenging, but there was also the fact that all the girls seemed a lot smarter than me, and there were certainly lots of more attractive men than me for them to choose from. As I saw it, this was not poor self esteem on my part, just a realistic evaluation of the situation at hand and an attempt to manage my own expectations.

But now, here I was in graduate school. The girls were even smarter, and there was even stronger male competition. Yet I was having a great time with this beautiful girl. (Maybe my self-confidence had improved a tiny bit.)

When we finished our dance, Carol said I was a good dancer. I told her I liked to dance a lot, but I didn't think I was very good, and I sure would like to take lessons someday. She said there was a place giving dance lessons right there at the university, and she wanted to take lessons too. We agreed in an instant that we would take lessons together! This was 1978, so of course the lessons we took were for disco dancing.

I suspect that our dance class experience was similar to most others: all the students stood at one end of the dance floor while the male and female teachers demonstrated the dance moves at the other end. Just like learning to ski, I had to make adjustments because I could not see any dance moves beyond six feet away. I explained my situation to the teachers and moved to within about three feet of them to watch their teaching.

by John H. Erickson

Even then, many of the moves weren't exactly what I thought they were, which sometimes lead Carol and I to dissolve into a tangle of arms and legs as we tried to move fluidly across the dance floor. That lead to a litany of "I'm sorry! I'm sorry!" from both of us. Finally, we agreed that there would always be two fundamental rules while dancing: Don't ever let go of your partner (because the visually impaired partner can't find you if you do). And dancing means never having to say you're sorry. (Take that, Ryan O'Neal!) We did concede that *oops* was acceptable and would work as a mild admission of guilt for a dance *faux pas*. Even today I advise all my dance partners of these precepts.

The key to really getting good on the dance floor is practicing over and over, hopefully with the same partner. And the man has to know how to lead! As a polite, well-mannered gentleman, I had always tried to dance while looking to my partner to see what she wanted to do next, and then trying to do it. I came to realize that this was as disastrous as trying to drive a car while looking for your passenger to make the next turn!

I have no doubt that the skills I learned in that dance class with Carol have been used more in the last 30 years than anything else I learned in class at Notre Dame or Northwestern! Not only have I done lots of dancing since those days, but I also apply the concepts generally and don't apologize for every slip-up in my life!

After our dance experience, Carol knew I was in need of readers for some of our class material, and she volunteered to do that too. She did start reading for me, and then we started spending more and more time together, and we ended up spending less and less time reading, until we weren't doing any reading at all.

Carol was my best friend at Northwestern. She was a great help with the classes, and our dancing together was some of the best times I've ever had. When I think back on all the good times at Northwestern, Carol is always in those memories.

SOMETIMES IT'S EASIEST NOT TO SAY ANYTHING

I remember one of my most challenging classes at Northwestern was a quantitative methods class that first semester. As had become policy with me, I introduced myself to the professor before classes started and explained my vision impairment and use of a Brailler in class.

A couple weeks later, however, the professor put a long equation up on the blackboard and explained it briefly. At the time, I was using markers and paper to write notes, not my Brailler, but I was unable to make any sense of the equation when I was done. I raised my hand and asked the professor to explain the equation again, but he replied in a voice that sounded somewhat frustrated, "It's right there on the chalkboard; it should be clear."

Huh, I thought. *He obviously doesn't remember that I can't see the board. If I remind him right here in class, in front of everyone, there could be unfavorable consequences.* So I just said thank you, and the class moved on. I made a special note to ask Carol and my roommate, Boots, whether they understood the equation, and most importantly, did they think it would be on the test!

Turns out nobody else understood the equation either, and it never appeared on a test. Discretion had been the better part of valor!

by *John H. Erickson*

A RESUME CONCERN

During my third quarter at Northwestern, the dean of the MBA program made a dramatic announcement: During a special assembly he informed us all that the name of the business school was about to change and become the Kellogg Graduate School of Management.

We had all applied to the Northwestern Graduate School of Management because of its great reputation, and we were all working hard to earn our MBA from that prestigious school. Now the dean was telling us we were not going to receive a diploma from the school we'd applied to, but from a school named after a brand of breakfast cereals. We were disappointed and dismayed, to say the least. Jokes were soon rampant that breakfast would be served 24 hours a day in the cafeteria, and Tony the Tiger and the Rice Krispie elves (Snap, Crackle, and Pop) would be featured on our diplomas.

Now instead of having a great grad school on my resume, I'd have to explain to prospective employers who the Kellogg Graduate School of Management was. Given my previous experiences with job interviews in the financial field, I did not feel I needed any additional obstacles.

Despite our feelings, the name was changed, so I did what seemed in my best self-interest: I ignored it! For several years, my resume said I'd graduated from the Northwestern Graduate School of Management, not Kellogg, and I strongly suspect that many of my classmates did the same. Fortunately for us, though, the reputation of Kellogg rose quickly, and I soon adjusted my resume for full accuracy. Today I am extremely proud to be a graduate of the first class of the Kellogg Graduate School of Management. The credentials and reputation of the school have proven to be enormous positives to my working career and beyond.

A FINE FINISH

During my MBA graduation ceremony, something happened I will never forget. As I'd done for both my high school and college graduations, I talked with the faculty in advance to be sure I knew the exact logistics of the ceremony so I wouldn't have to use my white cane. I didn't want to call any attention to my impaired vision, but not because I was embarrassed about it. I just didn't want to act like I had achieved more than any of my classmates. And I wanted to avoid any accidents.

So, to prepare for my Kellogg graduation, I went to the ceremony location and learned I would need to follow another student to a point at the front of the stage, then make my way across the stage to receive my diploma. After that I would continue across the rest of the stage to a wall, turn left, find the handrail, and go down four stairs to exit. Seemed like that would work just fine. No need for my white cane.

On the day of the graduation, the commencement speaker asked everyone to hold their applause until the end of the ceremony. Well, everyone did until it was my turn to cross the stage. As I did, I heard a small burst of applause. *Oh no*, I thought. My parents had already told me how proud they were, but this was obviously my family showing me their support one more time. I appreciated their enthusiasm, but I was embarrassed and a little miffed that my "supporters" had been the ones to violate the graduation protocol.

After the event was over, my dad asked how I felt about the graduation. I told him it felt great, but I did share that I'd been a bit embarrassed to hear the family clapping when I got my diploma.

"That wasn't us!" he said, a little defensively. "Those were your classmates!"

I was speechless for a long time after that. I've never received another award or recognition that meant more to me than their applause did, and I don't think I ever will.

THE ROAD TO EMPLOYMENT

At the end of my year at Kellogg, it was again time to interview for jobs. I now had both an undergraduate and graduate degree related to finance, and I again interviewed with any company that appeared to have anything to do with the industry. Ultimately, I still had no idea if I would be successful at getting a job because of my vision. So I deliberately set the bar of expectations very low.

My objective was to find a job—any job—that would pay me enough to live independently. I knew I was a prudent spender and very good saver, so I was not concerned with expectations for advancement or apprehensive that I would not enjoy the job. I just needed to make money to live, not to enjoy myself! Enjoying myself was what I hoped to do when the work day was over. If I found a paying job that I also enjoyed, that would be pure gravy.

For one of my many interviews, I talked with a municipal bond salesman from the John Nuveen company. At the end of our interview, he said he thought I was smart and a very nice guy, but he didn't know how I would ever do this job with my limited eyesight.

I just said I understood where he was coming from and left it at that. Today I realize I should have told him about all the technology available that would enable me to do it. I should have pointed out that he probably also didn't know just how I had lived on my own for the past five years and achieved both an undergraduate and graduate degree in finance!

Although this man did not offer me a job, he must have truly seen some potential in me because he did recommend that I contact a man named Don Bonniwell.

Don Bonniwell, "Bonny" to his friends, had been in the municipal bond industry for many years and had become blind during that time. He'd continued to work after this occurred and had become quite a success.

Wow! Finally here was someone with a visual impairment who had succeeded in finding a great job. I definitely wanted to meet him and find out how he had accomplished so much in the sighted world.

I got Mr. Bonniwell's telephone number and called him soon after that interview. We met, and he gave me some great advice. He recommended that I look for a job in the municipal bond industry because "munis" were bought and sold "over the counter." This meant transactions were done over the phone and not through an electronic exchange, so there were no screens or tapes to watch, and my limited eyesight would not be a negative. He also recommended that I steer my job search to companies on the "buy side" of the muni bond market, or those that bought municipal bonds—like bank trust departments, insurance companies, and mutual funds—rather than applying to large investment companies looking for salesmen to sell stocks and bonds. This way, I would be in a position where salesmen would do all the watching and searching for the bonds I wanted to buy. It was extremely good advice!

I took Bonny's recommendations and soon had an

interview with the trust department at the First National Bank of Chicago. Shortly after that, I had a job!

I know Bonny had a lot to do with me getting my first job there, as he had a strong relationship with that institution. I would spend a lot of time talking to municipal bond salesmen on the phone and making decisions about which bonds to buy. I had stumbled across the perfect industry for me!

MAKING A MOVE

After graduating in May, my job at the First National bank of Chicago would start in August 1979. Pete, now finished with his degree, was going to go to work full time for Dad in the trade show and convention business. Pete's degree in architecture, with its focus on space and design, was a perfect fit for laying out trade shows and conventions, and Pete had discovered that finding a true architecture job was very difficult. Dad welcomed the prospect of hiring someone that knew well the rigors of traveling and scheduling a trade show or convention.

But before "real life" began, Pete and I had decided we were going to celebrate the end of school with a five-week trip to Europe. We both had a little bit of school money left, and we had jobs lined up, so it was time to go nuts!

Neither of us had a new place to live, but that could wait until we returned from traveling. In the meantime, we stored all our stuff at our family home in River Forest.

On June 18, 1979, five of us left from Chicago and flew to London to begin a journey around Europe. Pete and me were joined by our high school friend Dick Mason, our sister Karen, and a friend of hers, Julie Fumo. Pete had made our trip itinerary and travel plans.

His itinerary took us from London to Amsterdam to Germany to Austria, and we ended our adventure in Rome, Italy. We traveled the whole way by train, often spending the night on board. Our accommodations were modest, and our dining included a lot more McDonalds than it probably should have, but the experience of traveling on our own and fending for ourselves—really for the first time ever—was fantastic.

As we traveled and saw the sights in each of the cities we visited, I used my white cane and moved right along with everyone else. I found that if I walked just one or two steps behind someone, I could tell if a step up or down was coming by watching the movement of their head and shoulders. If I did this, no one had to stop and say, "There's a step coming." every time we crossed a street or entered a restaurant. My walking and other movements became fluid and confident.

I also learned that travel by train and air were easy because the travel staff were eager to lend assistance when asked. I think that's when I truly got rid of all remnants of that male tendency not to ask for directions!

Pete, the most accomplished traveler among us, taught us the trick of boarding a train in Europe and securing a whole compartment for just our party. Because most passengers were either carrying suitcases or wearing large backpacks (like we were), the movement of people boarding the train and finding a seat was slow and cumbersome. Pete's method (which he'd learned while traveling in college with his archie buddies) was that one person left all their luggage with the group, sprinted onto the train, and found the first empty compartment. This person would shut the door quickly and then open the window. The rest of us would pass our luggage in through the window, which made the compartment appear totally full of people and secured our spots until we could make our way there through the crowd.

Dick kept a journal of the whole trip and made an entry near the end that he called "Most Often-Heard Comments." Looking back, the comments he recorded from both Pete and me were perfect indications of our future careers—Pete's in trade show and convention management and mine in wealth management. Pete was often heard saying, "You guys wait here, and I'll take care of everything." Whereas my most often heard comment was, "I think you still owe me some money from…"

When we got back from our trip, I had only weeks until my job started downtown. I had to get serious about finding a new place to live. I decided my new place had to be no more than 45 minutes from my new job, and all traveling had to be by mass transit. The obvious choice was somewhere in downtown Chicago, not too far from the Loop, Chicago's core business area where my new job was located.

I found a couple ads for small apartments right on Michigan Avenue, about six to eight blocks from where I'd be working, but when I went to check them out I was shocked to find that an apartment that met my criteria would cost me $400 a month—and that was an efficiency apartment with no bedrooms! Senior year at Notre Dame, Pete, Joe, and I had had a two-bedroom apartment for $300 a month. Now, just like Dorothy and Toto, I knew I wasn't in Kansas anymore. Still, $400 a month for a no-bedroom place seemed like highway robbery to me, and I wasn't going to get ripped off like that! (The reality was that I was totally out of touch with what downtown apartments cost!)

There was no money left in my pocket after my trip, so I moved back home. And funny thing, once I decided to do that, Pete figured he would too. We decided we'd stay just long enough to shop around and find something at a reasonable price. At least, that was our plan.

However, as often happens, living at home got way too comfortable for us, and the intensity of our searching for new places to live quickly faded. At our family home in River Forest, Pete was just three blocks from his office, and I was 35 to 40 minutes on the train from my job downtown. But even though Pete and I were living at home, we came and went as if we were on our own. About a year later, the inevitable happened when I went out for the night and didn't come home. The details are fuzzy, but suffice it to say, I went to a party downtown and woke up the next morning, still downtown. Soon after that Dad informed us it was time to move out!

So now we did the serious apartment shopping we'd been putting off, and each of us found a one-bedroom condo in Oak Park, about a mile from each other.

I lived in that condo for six years. It was there that I learned to cook for myself, pay all my own bills, and also discovered the basics of home insulation and weather-stripping as the Chicago winters in the early 1980s were some of the coldest on record! I even became a volunteer for Habitat For Humanity and learned that fixing and repairing a lot of things around the house was simple trial and error, not anything complicated or dangerous for a visually inconvenienced person. This knowledge continues to serve me well.

by John H. Erickson

IF YOU CAN'T SEE HOW TO FIT IN, ASK SOMEBODY

However, my first couple of years at the bank were more tough love, not at all easy or touchy feely. My job was to sit behind the municipal bond trading desk and pretty much do anything anyone else needed and did not want to do themselves. This made me the "Muni Go-For," but despite the challenges, I did not mind this one bit. I was so pleased to have a job and be learning about a whole industry I knew nothing about.

Dressing appropriately for my position was not something anyone talked to me about, and I started in the middle of August, when Chicago weather was at its hottest. To prepare for the transition from school to the working world, I had gone to your basic suit store and purchased two new suits that looked nice to me, one blue and one gray. Both were moderately priced polyester numbers, and I also got some short-sleeved white shirts to go along with them. These seemed to me to be nice additions to the blue, gray, and light brown suits I already had.

Within the first month or two of working, one of my female colleagues obviously took pity on me and quietly told me that if I did not want to be known as the "Prince of Polyester" around the office, I needed to spend some real bucks and buy some nice suits.

Not long after that, I walked into the office one hot summer day, wearing one of my short-sleeved white shirts, when the head of our Money Market area shouted across the room to me, "Hey, Elbows, what's with the short-sleeved shirts?" (However, he used much more colorful language than that.)

Until these cringe-worthy moments, I hadn't known that wearing long-sleeved shirts at the bank and avoiding polyester suits were absolutes, no matter what the weather outside was like.

Both these experiences were embarrassing, but I was glad they happened so I could fix the problems. There were no classes at Notre Dame or Northwestern called Proper Business Attire, but I sure could have used one! Anyway, it seemed proper business attire for a man in the First National Bank of Chicago's Trust Department in 1979 was a long-sleeved cotton shirt under a non-polyester suit. So I went and bought exactly those. And it should be noted that Glenn Wozniak, the money market manager who called me Elbows, became my best friend at First Chicago during those early years.

ALWAYS ASSUME OTHERS ARE WATCHING

Very soon after I started this first job, the most awkward event of my working career occurred—the result of someone watching me and my adaptive technology.

In the trading room, the three muni bond traders sat side by side along a large telephone bank, each with their own set of phones and direct lines. I was assigned to a desk behind them, with my face toward the wall and my back to theirs. I felt my setup was very private, and I had arranged my primary piece of adaptive technology, my CCTV, against the wall so its image faced me and the backs of the traders.

I opened my mail one day and was trying to make sense of an internal document addressed to me when Lois, one of the muni traders seated behind me, let out a short scream! I immediately turned around to see what the problem was, but she had stood up and was making her way out of the room. I asked what had happened, but no one else seemed to know what the problem was either.

So I turned back around and tried again to decipher just exactly what I was looking at on my CCTV screen, and I suddenly realized what had made Lois scream. I was staring at my first paycheck, which was now magnified 10 or 12 times and was easy for anyone to read if they glanced over my shoulder. And a nice paycheck it was! This check was more money than I had ever expected to receive from my very first job, and it was obviously more money than Lois ever expected the brand new, know-nothing grunt to receive.

Well, Lois and I never became close chums on the trading desk, but I got over the embarrassment of the whole episode pretty quickly, and I hope she did too. Since then I've always been careful not to put confidential information under my enlarger when others are nearby.

BLIND. *RIIIIGHT.*

But that's not to say I've completely eliminated misunderstandings and mishaps where my adaptive technology is concerned. Probably the most memorable experience I've ever had regarding this sort of confusion was at Wrigley Field during a Cubs game on a particularly cold day in April 1980.

I was there with a group of friends and excused myself to go to the men's room. I had already been there with someone else, so I knew exactly how to get there from where our seats were. I had memorized the sequence of left and right turns, as well as how many steps there were in each sequence. (This was my "mental breadcrumbs" trick I'd been using since high school.)

So I left our seats with my white cane and went to the steps to go back into the concession/bathroom area of the field. I started down that stairway with my white cane in one hand and the handrail, which ran down the middle of the steps, in the other. I could tell there was someone at the bottom starting up the stairs on the other side of the handrail, but I couldn't see them well enough to tell anything about them.

I went down several steps from the top and that person came up several stairs from the bottom. As we got closer and they became a little more clear to me, it looked like they were wearing two-tone pants—one color from the waist to the knee and another from the knee on down. *Wow*, I thought. *What peculiar pants.* I took another step down, they took another step up, and I glanced at them again. I noticed now that the person actually appeared to be wearing shorts, not pants. *It's freezing cold out here*, I remember thinking. *Who in their right mind would ever wear shorts to a Cubs game in April?*

As the person passed me on the stairs, I turned my head and glanced one more time just to confirm they really were wearing shorts. They were, as I reached the bottom of the stairs, I paused and thought to myself, *There really are some crazy people around here.* I glanced back up to the top of the stairs and saw the silhouette of the person standing there, looking back at me, hands on their hips.

"Blind. *Riiiiight*," I heard a sarcastic woman's voice say.

The other person on the stairs had been a woman, and she thought I'd been checking her out! That had not been the case at all, but that was way too much to try to explain, so I said nothing. I just turned my palms up, shook my head, and walked away.

OTHERS WANT TO HELP, SO LET THEM

Because my loss of eyesight had occurred during

adolescence, when I was naturally trying to become more independent, I had never been very good at asking for help when I needed it, and I was often resistant to those who offered it. If I thought I could do something without the help of others, I wanted to do it myself, both for my own satisfaction and to show those around me what I could accomplish.

When I started working after grad school, I was living in River Forest again, so I had a twice-daily commute of 45 to 60 minutes from home to work and back. The trip was pretty identical day after day, so I felt safe and comfortable doing it after a very short time.

I think it was a couple months after I'd started working when the first person approached me on the street and asked if they could help me cross. I know I was pretty quick to say, "Thank you, but no. I'm just fine." And I didn't think much more about it.

This sort of encounter happened every so often for several years until one time I heard what sounded like an elderly woman ask me if she could help me across the street. After I replied with my usual "Thank you, no. I'm just fine," I heard her say, "Oh, I see," in what sounded like a very disappointed voice. Something in that disappointed way she answered stuck in my mind.

Not very long after that, I was crossing another busy street in downtown Chicago when another woman asked if I needed help. For some reason, I didn't automatically reply with my standard "No, thank you," but thought to myself, *Why not? That would be nice.*

I said, "Thank you, I'd appreciate that." I took her arm, and we crossed the street.

When we got to the other side, before I could thank her,

she said thank you to me! Her remark took me by surprise, and I think I stammered something like, "Uh, thank you too!"

She seemed as grateful to me as I was to her. Why would that be? I tried to imagine the situation from a vantage point other than my own. There was no doubt in my mind that I stood out in a crowd, every morning and evening, making my way back and forth to the train from work.

If I ever came across someone with a different physical inconvenience than mine, like someone in a wheelchair, I would think about offering them assistance, but I would very likely talk myself out of it for any one of a thousand reasons. And if I did offer to assist that person, and they declined, I'd probably feel stupid that I'd asked in the first place!

What if my declining people's help had made them feel that way all these years? What if my declining a person's assistance had discouraged them from helping someone else the next time the opportunity came? I felt terrible, and I felt stupid that I had not considered the other point of view until now.

After that I never, ever refused someone's offer to assist me. I figure maybe if a person helps me and feels appreciated for doing so, they might be encouraged to do it again, perhaps for someone who could really, really use it.

Now I use those opportunities to inform people, if necessary, of the recommended way to assist a visually impaired person across the street. The person offering the help should never grab the VIP's arm and pull or push them across the street. Instead they should offer their forearm (between the elbow and wrist) to the VIP to hold. If the VIP seems to be totally blind, it helps if the person offering assistance pauses at the curb, both going down and coming up.

by John H. Erickson

DON'T ASK, DON'T GET

My starting job title at First Chicago was Assistant Municipal Trader. As the first several years of my career went by, I received favorable job reviews and small raises. My job responsibilities grew as I accomplished existing tasks and proved myself willing and able to take on new tasks on the trading desk. But I couldn't help but notice that my peers, the other MBAs that had started at the bank the same time I did, were all being promoted—first to Trust Officers and then Assistant Vice Presidents, and I just remained an Assistant Trader.

These other MBAs had begun their careers as either Assistant Portfolio Managers (working with the Portfolio Managers who worked with the actual clients of the Trust Department), or they were Assistant Equity Analysts, researching stocks for the Trust Department to buy for our clients. Being promoted from Assistant Portfolio Manager or Equity Analyst to Trust Officer did not necessarily change one's daily responsibilities, but it meant a whole new job grade and a significant increase in salary.

I did not want their jobs; I was really enjoying my own, and I kept assuring myself I was making a very good living and should be content with that. But when my fifth year with the bank came and went, I realized that just doing a good job was not going to get me promoted. My boss was not going to recognize that I was a good worker and reward my efforts with a promotion. So I went to the Human Resources Department and got a request for transfer form. I filled it out, saying I wanted to move off the trading desk and become an Assistant Portfolio Manager.

When I submitted the form to my boss for his signature,

he seemed surprised that being promoted and making more money was important to me! As hard as that was for me to believe, I also realized I had never spelled it out during any of my annual reviews.

He talked me out of submitting the transfer, and I was made a Trust Officer the very next quarter. I couldn't help but wonder if I would have gotten this promotion years earlier if I'd just spoken up. And I made a huge note to self about this: Never hesitate to spell out exactly where you want to go and what you want to achieve during reviews and other opportunities. It's not being pushy or not being appreciative of what you have. It's more likely considered complacent if you don't do it! Just like interviewing, you have to spell out what you want and why you deserve it. No bragging, just facts!

DON'T CORRECT, EDUCATE

By the early 1990s, I had worked my way up on the municipal bond trading desk and now managed all the municipal bond funds for the Wealth Management Department (formerly the bank's Trust Department). I was getting ready to go out to lunch one day when I got a call that the new Chief Investment Officer (CIO) wanted to see me and a couple of the other security traders in his office. Figuring I would leave for lunch right after the meeting was over, I grabbed my collapsible white cane and went to his office.

When the other security traders and I went in, the CIO saw the cane in my hand and said, "Are you taking an umbrella with you today? I don't think you'll need it. It's not supposed to rain."

I realized he didn't recognize my collapsible white cane,

and may not have known I was visually impaired, though everyone else in the room did. I knew they were likely waiting anxiously to hear how I was going to answer. Obviously this was a very different situation than my run-in with the woman in the park many years earlier. "Oh, that's an easy mistake to make," I told him. "This is my collapsible white cane, and it does look just like an umbrella!"

This was definitely the right way to answer, and the conversation quickly changed topics. When the small group of us finished the meeting with the CIO, we went on to lunch. I heard later that the CIO had been thoroughly embarrassed about the incident, but he was able to joke about it.

As luck would have it, I read an article in the paper about a week later about a legally blind man in California who was standing at a bus stop with a collapsible white cane in his back pocket. An off-duty police officer saw the white cane and thought it was some kind of weapon. He approached the man and told him to empty his pockets. The man did not know who was asking him to empty his pockets, so he refused. A scuffle ensued, and the off-duty police officer wrestled the man to the ground, only to discover he was visually impaired and had a cane in his pocket, not any kind of weapon. I cut out the article and sent it to my CIO with a note. "See, no worries," I wrote. "Lots of other people don't know what a collapsible white cane is either!"

Chapter 6:   A Life of Faith

THE ROLE OF FAITH

As I look back over my life—or my two lives, actually—I can trace the path I followed in coming to terms with my visual impairment. I can also see the journey my spiritual life has taken me on. My developing understanding of God and His plan for my life has been another huge factor in making me the person I am today.

Way back when Pete and I were little kids, our family regularly attended St. Luke's Catholic Church in River Forest, and we grew up with regular prayers at meals and bedtime. I found the precepts and teachings of the church in perfect harmony with both school and home life. Namely, like my teachers and parents, God also rewarded good behavior (most of the time), and He quite often punished bad behavior, although mostly in the stories of the Old Testament.

My earliest evaluations of Jesus were that He either decided Himself (or was coerced by God the Father) to come to Earth and teach us all the things the prophets had failed to explain well, and eventually He died on the cross to offset what the nuns called "Original Sin." Original Sin guaranteed that none of us humans could be perfect and slide easily into heaven, regardless of how good our actions were here on Earth.

So, as I figured it, Jesus had to come to Earth to die on the cross so we could get past Original Sin and be judged by God on the merits of our own lives. I knew I wasn't alone in this belief, either. In one of my favorite songs as a kid, "Last Kiss," by J. Frank Wilson, the singer lamented the loss of his "baby" and pledged to be good so he could see her again in heaven someday. To me, the church offered a very clear framework of dos and don'ts that I could use as guidelines in my life.

The one unsettling thing that occurred quite often, though, was that I would see others clearly violate these rules and regulations, and they would not only get away with it, but the powers that be would not even seem to care. Still, I stuck with the rules anyway. This was perhaps because I was a better follower than independent thinker during the early years of grade school.

For many years, this integration of home life, school, and church was seamless and easy. However, as I grew older, heard more Scripture at church, and became familiar with more and more passages, inconsistencies started to pop up. There were passages in the Bible that did not back up my beliefs that God rewarded good behavior and punished bad. The stories I remember being the most puzzling were the parable of the prodigal son, the workers in the field, and the stewards and the talents. They just did not seem fair.

In the parable of the prodigal son (Luke 15:11-32), one son is obedient to his father, while the other acts like a selfish, self-centered, ungrateful brat and asks his father to give him the inheritance that will someday be coming to him. Then the son takes off and squanders the money. When he has nothing and is left suffering, he comes to his senses and realizes what a jerk he's been. He decides to return home and ask his father if he can work for him. When he gets there, his father sees him coming and runs to greet him. Then the father orders that a party be thrown in the son's honor.

Seeing all this happen, the other son, who has always been obedient to his father, is justifiably upset. He says to the father, "Hey, what gives? I've worked hard for you and done everything you've asked, unlike this brother of mine, and you've never thrown a party for me!"

The father tells the son not to worry about it, that he will reward him someday, but for now everyone should rejoice because the other son was lost but has returned to them. Scripture never says anything more about how the good son took that explanation, but it always seemed lame to me. It clearly did not fit into my fundamental beliefs about being rewarded for good behavior and not rewarded for bad.

In the parable of the workers in the field (Matthew 20:1-16), the owner of the field hires workers throughout the day, but pays them all exactly the same amount when the day is over. In the parable of the talents, (Matthew 25:14-30) the wealthy master gives each of three stewards different amounts of money and gets mad at the one who received the smallest amount because he does not invest it wisely.

Luckily, I was able to put the cognitive dissonance these stories created aside by deciding they must be among those mysteries that humans aren't supposed to understand.

Based on my understanding of God and the world around me, I never believed my vision problems were some kind of retribution for poor or unsatisfactory behavior. It was pretty easy to look around and see others who were not following the rules as well as I was! And if that was not enough, the newspaper and evening news included the stories of tons of others who were off the charts with bad behavior.

Some time during our sophomore year of high school, Pete and I were invited to a Young Life meeting by a couple of our friends. Young Life is a non-denominational Christian youth group that has weekly meetings at people's houses. The meetings were about an hour long and consisted of about half an hour of singing, 15 or so minutes of skits and funny stuff, and a message about Jesus at the end. This was unlike any religious activity I had ever participated in, and I really liked it. The music was beautiful, as the singing was dominated by the girls there, and the skits were often slapstick in nature—totally different from church.

Our family continued to regularly attend church at St. Luke's during high school, and Pete's and my participation in Young Life with our friends did not mean that our time at the Catholic church was cut back at all. Going to church as a family was important to everyone in my family. But Young Life was my first glimpse of how other Christians live their lives, so I was very interested. Here was a place where you could have fun and laugh and still be participating in something spiritual. Prior to this, I'd felt that anytime I found myself having lots of fun, I was probably doing something wrong. The final messages at Young Life always had a Jesus focus to them, and I became interested in learning more about why friends and acquaintances from other Christian denominations did not seem to have as structured or rigorous a formula for living life.

During the summer between junior and senior year, I found myself in the mountains of Colorado at a Young Life camp, listening to one of the leaders make his final points on a very emotional sermon regarding Jesus and his death on the cross. "I want each of you to ask yourself: Are you a Christian?" he said. I thought deeply and sincerely answered to myself, "I'm sure trying to be." Then the leader said, "And if you say to yourself, 'I'm trying to be'—then you're not!"

Well, I was stunned and devastated at the same time. How could he say that? I was so upset that I stopped listening to whatever else he had to say. The speaker that night very well may have gone on to do a fine job of explaining what he meant, but I heard none of it. We were soon excused from the talk and encouraged to find a place by ourselves and pray or ponder what we'd heard. I did so and prayed to God that "I did not get at all this idea of 'not trying to be a Christian.' How could any of us ever get to heaven and be with God and Jesus if we never tried?" But I also prayed that God would help me figure out what all this was supposed to mean.

I would not find that answer for about six years.

THERE'S A REASON FOR EVERYTHING

A year or so after I started working, when I was 24, I got a call from a girl named Beth Phillips. Beth was a friend of Jules Mason, the wife of my best high school friend, Dick Mason. Beth and I had first met at Dick and Jules' wedding just a few months earlier, and she was calling to invite me to go with her to a singles Bible study up on the north side of Chicago called The Hub. I accepted immediately, but it wasn't because I was interested in any kind of bible study; Beth was very attractive, and she was a blond.

The Hub met in the early evening at the Salvation Army office near Wrigley Field. The program consisted of an opening with music and then a lesson taught by the guest speaker. I enjoyed that first visit very much, but I realized that The Hub was just too far away from home for me to attend on a regular basis. It would mean taking public transportation for well over two hours round trip each time I came. Also, I quickly realized Beth's intentions were simply to introduce me to The Hub. She did not have any romantic interest in me at all.

Before the meeting was over, another girl came up and introduced herself as Judy Beyer. Judy said she and I had been classmates during high school, and she remembered me from her creative writing class. She added that she didn't expect me to remember her because she had been a very quiet person during high school. She told me she lived in Oak Park now and would be willing to give me a ride to and from The Hub anytime I wanted.

The very next week, Judy called and offered to drive me to The Hub that night, if I was going. I had enjoyed my first visit, so I took her up on her offer. In no time, Judy and I were going to The Hub on a regular basis.

One of the first lessons I participated in at The Hub was a study of the book of Romans. As the lesson progressed, I began to feel as though the teacher somehow knew about my episode in Colorado at the Young Life camp, because he proceeded to methodically address the list of conflicts that had arisen that night about five years earlier.

First, the Hub speaker went to Romans 3:23. "For all have sinned and fall short of the glory of God." No one, no one at all, is good enough to earn their way into heaven. Original sin, or simply human nature, totally stops us from ever being able to earn our way there.

Then the speaker went to Ephesians 2:8, 9. There Scripture says, "For it is by grace you have been saved, through faith. And this is not from yourselves. It is the gift of God, so no one can boast." God's grace—the gift of Jesus as a sacrifice for all sins—is what opens heaven to mankind, not any kind of list of good works that we do ourselves.

This is what explains the parables of the prodigal son and the workers in the field. No matter how much work or good things we do here on Earth, it doesn't add up to a ticket to heaven. We do whatever we can here just because God loves us so much and we love Him back. Maybe that's not how you or I would set things up, but God's ways aren't our ways!

As far as my objection that salvation couldn't be that easy, the speaker pointed out that there was nothing easy about Jesus dying on the cross. It was truly a painful and horrific death, and it showed the incredible magnitude of God's love for us. "For God so loved the world that He gave His only Son…that we may have eternal life." (John 3:16)

So, if you believe that Jesus is the Son of God (and I did), and you are truly sorry for your sins (and I was), then not to believe your salvation is assured through Jesus's death and resurrection is to be at the foot of the cross and either say, "Nice gesture, Jesus, but that's not enough for me." or "No thanks, Jesus. I want to get to heaven on my own good works."

I wasn't going to say either of those things! So I kept coming back to The Hub to learn more about what Scripture said. Coming early and helping to move chairs became very much a part of my experience there. I wasn't familiar enough with Scripture to help with any of the teaching, but I was very good at moving tables and chairs.

During one of my early visits, a leader asked me if I would open the evening with the prayer.

"No, I'm sure there are much more qualified people around to open in prayer," I said.

The leader said fine and moved on, but I felt so guilty

about saying no, that I started to listen carefully to others who were praying so I could piece together a prayer of my own. Not long afterward, I volunteered to open the meeting in prayer, and successfully did so!

I was feeling pretty proud of myself for coming through with that opening prayer, but soon after that I came across the Scripture that says, "Don't worry about what you will say before men, the Holy Spirit will help you." And he did!

Sometime later, I came across the Scripture passage that would come to be my very favorite: John 9:1-3. It's the story of Jesus and his disciples coming across a blind man. The disciples ask if the man is blind because of his own sins or the sins of his father.

"Neither this man nor his parents sinned," said Jesus. "But this happened so that the work of God might be displayed in his life."

Wow, there it was. An explanation that made so much sense about the purpose of my loss of sight. God had done amazing things in my life, but I needed to have the experience of losing my sight to see that. I also began to see that God had many, many more blessings in store for me, and my sight loss was necessary for those things to happen.

If God is love, then God's work is love, and if the blind man in the parable lost his sight so that the love of God might be displayed, then it truly made sense to me that that's why I had lost my sight too.

Today, what Scripture says about God's plan for each of us seems a lot clearer and not so filled with contradictions as it first seemed to me. It's amazing how God brought me to The

Hub and how He used Beth and Judy to keep me there long enough to learn what I needed to know.

The Hub also introduced me to a new concept I hadn't heard of before: the idea that each of us should look for a mate who was "equally yoked" to God—someone at a similar place in their faith. As I saw it, this was an additional roadblock to finding the girl who would become my wife. It wasn't like I had the luxury of being able to narrow the universe of eligible spouse candidates. My life at that time was not some kind of High Karate aftershave commercial where I was fighting off women! Reluctantly though, I decided I would keep the idea in mind and see how it went.

Chapter 7:   A Life Partner

OPPORTUNITIES IN UNSUSPECTED PLACES

For the next several years, during the early 1980s, my work at First Chicago kept me very busy. I took on more and more responsibility as others in my department left to take new opportunities. I often stayed a little after work to clean up loose ends and prepare for the next day.

In the midst of all that, making arrangements to meet and set dates with women proved to be a difficult task. As I had discovered in high school, I could not spot a girl at a distance and decide whether she was the type I was going to go after. And conversely, because I couldn't see them, I couldn't respond to a girl who might spot me and try to drop some kind of visual sign that she was interested, like a wink or a smile.

I know for a fact that I missed at least one opportunity that way. A young woman who worked in another area of the bank met me at several municipal bond functions where I was not using my white cane. She knew I was a nice guy, and I assume she thought I was okay looking, so she would smile and wave at me when our paths crossed in the lobby or cafeteria of the bank, also times when I was not using my white cane. Of course, I did not see her, so I appeared to ignore her totally.

One day she shared with another co-worker these experiences and her frustration that I was acting like such a jerk and ignoring her. The co-worker, who knew me better, just started laughing. "He's legally blind," she finally explained. "He can't see you!"

Luckily, the woman had a great sense of humor and was the type of person who eventually felt comfortable enough to share the story with me. We laughed about it together, and last I heard, she's married and lives in Florida.

With challenges like this, I had to focus on opportunities when I was thrown together with available women. This led to a little remorse that I hadn't made better use of the opportunity Notre Dame had offered me to meet girls. And if you are narrowing the universe of candidates to those who are Christians, the task gets even harder!

Nevertheless, after later analysis, I can say that the Bible is true: "All things work for the good for those who believe." (Romans 8:28)

In 1984, the American Blind Skiing Foundation began taking annual trips to well-known ski resorts, and the first they chose was Banff, Canada! This sounded like an exotic destination and a trip of a lifetime, so I signed up immediately.

When the trip came along in March, we stayed at beautiful accommodations—The Banff Springs Hotel—and had the unique opportunity to meet up with a group of Canadian visually impaired skiers who happened to be there at the same time. We had a pizza dinner together and then hung around and played board games, like Trivial Pursuit. When the game-playing began, I was captivated by one of the Canadian skiers.

Her name was Brenda, and her fun, friendly, and confident personality drew me like a magnet. A short time later, we found ourselves dancing.

"Oh, it's so refreshing to dance with a man who knows how to lead," she told me. No one had complimented me like that in a very long time, so this girl was building up all kinds of great marks in my book! But it was the next thing she said that knocked my socks off. "You're a Christian, aren't you?" she added.

I think I stammered something like, "Uh, yeah, but how did you know?"

"Oh, it shows," she said.

That may have been the greatest compliment I had ever received, and I had to know more about this woman. When we finished dancing, I asked her where she was going to be skiing the next day because I wanted to meet her for lunch, coffee—any reason I could think of!

"Our group is leaving in the morning," she said, and my heart sank.

NO!!! a silent voice inside me shouted. So I talked her into meeting me for breakfast before they left. She brought a friend with her, so I didn't share all the feelings I had experienced the night before. But I began making plans to visit Brenda as soon as I returned to Chicago, and I soon flew to Edmonton, Alberta, to see her.

I thought the visit went well, but I played it cool again because I had an enormous fear that I might come on too strong and scare her away. After all, she was a graduate student finishing up her studies, and I was just this foreign guy she had met on a ski trip!

A short time after that visit, Brenda wrote and told me she just wanted to be friends. Though initially disappointed, I decided I was okay with that, and Brenda is still a good friend of mine today.

I realize now that I had to travel 1,600 miles away from home to see a glimpse of what I was looking for in a partner. But I would find the right partner very soon!

A BLIND DATE FOR A BLIND GUY MAKES PERFECT SENSE

In the summer of 1984, I received a save-the-date announcement for my 10-year high school reunion coming up in the fall. I had attended a grade-school reunion several years earlier and had a great time, so I decided I would go to the high school reunion too. But I didn't think about it much after that. The prospects of meeting someone there I didn't already know, and a Christian to boot, seemed slim to none.

A month or two before the reunion, I was talking with a high school classmate of mine, Al Peyton. Al and his wife, Liz, lived in Oak Park and were going to the reunion too. Al asked me if I already had a date and said he and Liz knew a girl from church they wanted to introduce me to. He thought the reunion would be a great opportunity for us to have a first date. However, I told Al I thought the whole plan was dumb. If I went to the reunion and had a good time with my old classmates, this girl might feel left out. Plus, this was the first time I was going to see many of these people in 10 years—I couldn't show up with just anyone as my date!

But Al was persistent. He said maybe all four of us could have a quick double date before the reunion so I could check this girl out. I decided that was not a bad idea. Her name was Jane Hatfield, and I took down her phone number to call her.

by John H. Erickson

She was from Camp Hill, Pennsylvania, a suburb of Harrisburg. She had come to Chicago to go to Wheaton College, where her mom had gone to college too. Jane and I had graduated from college the same year, and she'd taken a job as a banker at American National Bank right out of school.

Jane lived in Wheaton for a short time after college, but she'd moved to Oak Park for a better commute downtown. Now she lived only three blocks away from me. That's what I call geographically desirable!

But Al beat me to the punch. He immediately called Jane after he and I talked and told her a friend of his would be calling her soon to ask her out. He went on to say that this friend lived in Oak Park, was a banker just like she was, and was a graduate of Notre Dame and Kellogg.

Then he asked Jane, "You would go out on a date with a guy like that, right?"

She said, "Well, sure, I guess."

"Great!," he said. "Liz and I are looking forward to it. Oh yeah, one last thing, my friend is blind. That's okay, right?"

Jane remembers thinking to herself, *Oh great, now what do I say?* But she said, "Oh, no problem. That's just fine."

As she hung up the phone, her roommate asked, "What was that all about?"

"I'm going on a blind date," Jane said. "No, I mean I'm going out with a date who's blind!"

Then she sat back and waited to hear from this mysterious blind guy.

When I finally got around to calling Jane, I asked her if she wanted to go to the movies on a double date with Al and Liz. There was a movie theater just a block away from where we lived, and I suggested we all meet right there. Jane said that would be fine, but she does remember thinking it was strange that a blind guy wanted to go to the movies!

Following my usual movie-viewing policy, Jane and I sat in the fifth row of the theater, then went back to my apartment for pizza with Liz and Al. When the date was over, I thought things had gone very well. Jane was really cute, friendly, smart, laughed at my jokes, and, yes, she was blond! So I took the next step and asked her to come to the reunion with me. Jane already knew several other friends of hers would be at the reunion, so she said yes to that too.

The reunion was lots of fun. Not only did I enjoy being with Jane, but I saw lots of old friends and former classmates. At the time, I thought I did a really nice job of balancing the reunion night between spending time with Jane and catching up with my old classmates. However, to this day, Jane likes to pull my chain when we talk about it. She tells people she didn't mind at all when girls kept coming up to her and saying, "You came with John Erickson. Do you know where he is?"

I wasn't totally clueless about what a nice thing it was that Jane put up with going to the reunion. Whether or not she and I were meant to be, I knew at the least I owed her some nice dinners out—that is, if she would ever go out with me again! But she did. We began spending more and more time together in the weeks and months after the reunion.

COMPLEMENTS ATTRACT

Jane and I started dating on a regular basis, and I found we had a lot more in common than just working for a bank. She was the oldest in her family, just like me, and her family had always been important to her, just like mine had to me.

But what really struck me and attracted me to her were all the things I wasn't good at that she did so well.

Jane was a detail person, something I had never been good at. She also had a remarkable way of listening to people and analyzing their wants and desires, getting past just what the person said. This was way beyond my skill set. I was okay with the Golden Rule, just doing unto others as I wanted them to do unto me, but Jane was a whole level higher than that. She would do unto others as they would want someone to do onto them.

This requires the ability to put yourself into another person's shoes, determine what they want, and accept that. I wasn't good at that at all. The best example of this is what I call "the cut-flower conundrum." I had always heard that girls liked bouquets of cut flowers, but this made no sense to me. Why would someone want to spend good money on something that was doomed to shrivel and die in just a few days? But Jane showed me that it didn't matter what I thought about the other person's desire; what mattered is what they wanted. When it came to this sort of stuff, I realized she could teach me a lot!

About three months after Jane and I started dating, I had plans to spend my two weeks of vacation doing some skiing in Colorado, then going to visit my old friend Betsy Kettlehut (from our summers at the cottage in Michigan), now Betsy Koepsel, and her husband, Ron. They had just moved to Boca Raton, Florida, from Chicago the prior year.

I found out that Jane had plans to visit her grandfather in Boca Raton, and our trips overlapped one weekend. So we made plans to rendezvous in Boca. Betsy, Ron, and I picked up

Jane at her grandfather's house and spent two nights seeing the sights in Boca. We had a great time, and then Jane left to go back to Chicago.

That evening, Betsy told me she thought Jane was great, and I should call and ask her to come back down to Boca the next weekend. I explained to Betsy that I thought that was a nice idea, but I already knew Jane was the kind of woman who was orderly and made her plans long in advance. It was doubtful she would just pick up and travel to Boca Raton on a minute's notice.

Betsy said, "Fine. Call her and check."

So I called Jane and invited her to come back down. Much to my surprise, she said she would check the airfares and call me back.

The next day, Jane called to say she had checked the flights back to Florida, and the only tickets available were first class, and the prices were way too high. When I conveyed this message to Betsy, she simply said, "Give Jane your credit card." So I did.

Much to my surprise, Jane took the card number over the phone and said she would book the flight.

Jane flew back that next weekend, and we had another fun time with Ron and Betsy. That little spontaneous excursion to Florida told me a lot about Jane I didn't know, and I liked it all! And I'm sure it told Jane a lot about me too.

Over the next nine months or so, Jane and I did lots of things together. For a while, we called each other every morning and did our daily devotions together. She met the rest of my family, and we flew to Harrisburg where I met hers too. Our offices in downtown Chicago were only three blocks apart, so we did our best to schedule lunches here and there.

by John H. Erickson

But both of us were very dedicated to our jobs, so we spent most of our time together after work.

I don't remember ever having any big discussions about my eyesight. What I loved so much about Jane was her never-ending positive attitude and her apparent enjoyment of being with me. I don't remember any awkward times of trying to figure out what she meant by a comment. She was so genuine. And her care for people was apparent too.

When the fall came and we'd been dating about a year, the light bulb in my head finally went on, and I realized Jane was the lifetime mate I was looking for. At Thanksgiving, we visited her parents, and I asked her dad for his blessing to marry her. Then it was time to decide when I was going to pop the question. I wanted a date that would be easy to remember, but Christmas and New Years seemed too obvious, and Super Bowl Sunday wasn't on the same day each year. So I chose Groundhog Day to propose.

That night, there was a James Bond movie on TV, so inviting Jane over was not suspicious. During a commercial, I turned the volume down and told her I had a Groundhog Day present for her. She unwrapped a medium-size box to find a small toy squirrel with a note in his hand. (Finding a groundhog stuffed animal was not as easy as I'd thought it would be!) The note said: My cousin the groundhog is very busy today, so I am delivering this message for him. John Erickson wants to marry you, and he wants to know if you will marry him! You can give him your answer directly.

Jane quietly read this note to herself, and I was delighted and relieved when she turned to me with a big smile and said yes.

We got married in July 1986 in Harrisburg, at Jane's childhood church. There are two things about our wedding I'll always remember. One, just a couple days before I left Chicago for the wedding, I cracked a small bone in my toe. By the morning of the wedding, my foot didn't hurt at all, but it had swollen so much that I couldn't fit into my tuxedo shoes. My dad came through for me again, as I ended up wearing his shoes for the wedding.

Second, as the ceremony began, I waited at the front of the church with my groomsmen. The music began playing as the bridal party came down the main aisle. All the bridesmaids made their way to the front of the church, one by one appearing to me through the fog of my eyesight. But there was no Jane following them. The music just kept playing, and I kept waiting for Jane to appear through the fog of my poor eyesight.

I found out later she was three-quarters of the way down the aisle, just out of my vision range, waiting for the photographer to reload his camera with film. But all that time I had stood at the front of the church wondering if she'd changed her mind about marrying me.

PLAY TO YOUR STRENGTHS

As we began our life together, although we were both bankers by career, we agreed that I would be the one responsible for saving and budgeting, while Jane would handle the day-to-day finances, as well as our social calendar. We've kept those jobs to this day. We both do our best to keep the other informed about our lives, and we've found that when one of us is depressed or down about something, the other can be uplifting and a reminder of how blessed our lives are.

Jane is outstanding at reading people and determining their concerns and needs, and I am not. We work well as complements to each other, which makes our match a great one. And when we've faced what appear to be irreconcilable differences, we pray about it and try to put any resolution in God's hands. This has worked every time.

EVERY ACHIEVEMENT MAKES ME FEEL LESS IMPAIRED

Beginning married life presented a whole new list of responsibilities and challenges. There were more errands to run and places to be, and Jane was the only one who could drive. I saw while we were dating that she liked to drive, and she never, ever complained that she had to do it all. She was exactly the same way when we got married. But it made me uneasy to feel that she was carrying more of our "being-married burdens" than I was.

So I felt even more driven to push the envelope and try to do things that weren't easy because of my vision. We lived in an apartment the first year we were married, but we moved to a small "starter home" after one year, complete with a front and back yard to mow. Both were pretty tiny, and there was no way I was going to pay a lawn service to mow them, so we bought a lawnmower, and I fired it up!

Just like when you build a jigsaw puzzle, I started around the outer edge of the lawn. I mowed all around the perimeter of the yard, and then I did it again, now trying to estimate one mower-width over from where I started. As I mowed, I couldn't really tell if I was mowing where I had already been or not, but it turned out that my system worked pretty well.

When I felt I had finished, Jane came out into the yard and finished mowing "the skippers" that had been left behind in my wake.

This worked so well that today I trim the bushes, rake the lawn, snow-blow and shovel the snow, do some painting, and a host of other things, always knowing that Jane will step to the plate and catch my "skippers" when I'm done.

FAMILY GUY

Our son, JP, was born in 1988, just over two years after we were married, and our daughter, Ellie, was born two and a half years later in 1991. I never could have imagined how wonderful it would be to be a father and bring up a family. Now that I know how much love I have for a child, I realize the true depth of God's love for His children defies our understanding.

When the kids were little, we tried to address my "bad eyesight" directly. As they got a little older, I even tried to put a positive spin on things. I did not want JP and Ellie to grow up with the same poor perception of what it meant to be blind, or visually impaired, that I'd had. I wanted them to know all the things a VIP *could* do, not imagine how terrible a life with impaired vision would be. So I offered to speak to their different grade school classes about being visually impaired, and I showed and demonstrated my cool aids and appliances for the students.

When JP was about five or six, Jane asked him what kind of car he was going to buy when he grew up. He told her very seriously that he was not going to drive when he grew up. He was going to have Allison (one of his friends) drive all the time, just like Jane did for me. Jane did her best to explain why that idea was probably not going to fly.

About that same time, JP made me aware of a peculiar habit. We were at the dinner table as a family one evening when the children were about five and three. One of Jane's most wonderful characteristics is her endless hospitality and related emphasis on manners and appropriate behavior. Both JP and Ellie had seemed to be coming along just fine with their manners, but as we were passing around the meat dish, JP picked up the salt shaker and proceeded to pour salt into the palm of his hand, then sprinkle it onto his plate.

Jane and I were appalled. We seemed to simultaneously tell JP things like, "You don't ever put your salt on your food like that!" and "You know better than that."

JP seemed a bit confused at our sudden and united objection to his behavior. "Dad does that all the time," he said.

I think I started laughing, suddenly recognizing the hypocrisy of my comments, and never thinking the kids paid attention to little things like that. But Jane took the high road. "Uh, well, sweetheart, that's because Dad can't see how fast the salt is coming out of the shaker."

JP simply said "Oh," and went back to eating.

After that I vowed to do a better job of explaining to the kids, and others, the reasons why I do things in peculiar ways to compensate for my impaired vision.

EVERYONE HAS BUMPS IN THE ROAD

In 1996, my life and my family seemed to be going great. My job at First Chicago was wonderful. I was running municipal bond funds now and had been recognized three times by the Lipper Analytical Service and by the American Banking Association for top performing funds in their category. I'd also achieved top performance over 10 years in the Nuveen Municipal Common Trust Fund report.

We had just moved to a bigger house in River Forest, and the kids were enjoying school there. Then, just as I'd started to feel comfortable with the idea of working at one place my whole career, First Chicago merged with NBD Bank in Detroit and moved the Investment Trading Unit of the Wealth Management Department there. I was invited to come, but Jane and I decided our lives were in Chicago now, and this was where we were going to stay.

So I had to face the unthinkable: voluntarily giving up a job I loved and finding a new one. Although this went against my whole essence, I saw the big picture for one of the first times, and I knew leaving the bank to stay in Chicago was the right thing to do. Fortunately, the bank had a fantastic severance program, which rewarded those like me who had stuck it out for so many years.

While I wasn't working, most weekdays I got up and went to the bank's outplacement office to research and find other job opportunities, but also did every personal summer activity I wanted to. This included being a Little League coach for JP's team, which was a great way to relive my great memories of being in Little League so many years ago.

After four months of having great fun, and still looking for that next job, I called one of my old colleagues at First Chicago, Jeff Roberts, to ask a question. When we spoke, he said he thought I'd found another position months ago. When I told him I hadn't, he got back to me with a job offer as an account manager within the Wealth Management Department, and I was delighted! Although the unit that traded securities had moved to Detroit, the people who had personal contact with clients had not, and now I was going to be a part of that group.

I returned to First Chicago for about eight months, but then I received a phone call from Mark Quinn, my former boss at the bank who had also been let go. Mark told me he had just finished an interview at LaSalle Bank, and they were specifically looking for someone with a lot of municipal bond experience. He thought I was the perfect person for that job.

Well, Mark was right. I spoke with LaSalle, and they hired me as Director of Fixed Income within the Wealth Management Department, and I worked for LaSalle for the next twelve years.

FURTHER LOSS

In early 2006, when I was 49 years old, another serious physical challenge came into my life when I began to lose my hearing. The loss was very subtle at first; there were just occasional times I had to ask Jane what she'd just said or ask clients to repeat themselves during a business meeting. At work, we had weekly meetings in a boardroom around a large table that sat about 24 people. Over time I began to notice that wherever I sat, I had difficulty understanding what the people farthest away from me were saying. The problem continued, so I went to an ear doctor to check it out.

The diagnosis came much more quickly than the reason for my eyesight problem had come so many years ago, but the prognosis was again rather bleak. It was premature hearing loss, and there was nothing they could do about it. There were no treatments or surgeries to fix it; I could only try to mitigate the loss with the use of hearing aids.

Long ago, when I had contemplated the possibility of

going totally blind, I'd thought sight would be the most serious sense to lose. But now I was convinced hearing would be the most difficult loss. Even Helen Keller once said, "When you lose your sight, you lose the world, but when you lose your hearing, you lose people." In a very short period of time, I saw that hearing loss was going to impact my life even more than becoming legally blind so many years ago.

The hearing issue came to a head later that year when I was with a group of guys from church. We had gathered in a large room, and one person raised his voice and said something I couldn't make out. Then the whole room broke out laughing. Someone else added a comment to what the first person had said, and the room erupted with laughter again. I was completely lost. I looked at my friends on either side of me and contemplated whether I should ask them what those first guys had said. But I quickly realized it was futile— no one could explain what had been said fast enough, before the next comment came out.

I was left with a feeling of despair. For most of my life, I had been the funny guy—cracking the jokes or coming back to someone with a zinger reply. My sense of humor had helped me so much as I coped with the loss of my eyesight. And I suddenly saw that whole part of my life vanishing before my eyes.

I would not be that funny guy any more. If I couldn't make out what people were saying, I would be the person who just sat there while others were talking, waiting for someone to tap me on the shoulder and speak loudly and slowly enough for me to understand what they wanted.

I felt my eyes starting to moisten, so I walked away from

the group, so no one would see my reaction. I regained my composure and returned to the group several minutes later, but the realization put me in a somber mood for several days.

Just a few months later, Jane, JP, Ellie and I were all together in a very crowded and noisy restaurant. Jane and the kids were ordering, and I was sitting the farthest away from the server. Jane leaned over to me and said something, but I couldn't make it out.

I said, "Sorry, what?"

"It's your turn to order!" she said again, louder, but with no particular indication that she was upset or frustrated with me.

However, I was suddenly overcome with a sense that I was now an embarrassment to my family. It took all my willpower to hold myself together and keep in my emotions, and I didn't say hardly anything for the rest of the meal.

When Jane and I were alone later, she asked me why I had been so quiet during the meal. The idea that I was now an embarrassment to Jane and the kids welled up inside me, and I totally lost my composure. When I had pulled myself together again, Jane assured me that this wasn't at all the case, and she and I resolved that I would immediately begin researching hearing aids and other technology to help my hearing.

I saw a couple audiologists as quickly as I could and got fitted with my first hearing aid within a couple weeks. I'd decided that functioning at work was my top priority, so I found hearing aids with a separate microphone that I could place at the opposite end of the large table at work to hear the others there during meetings. I also found the microphone helpful when I was meeting with clients.

Those first hearing aids and separate microphone weren't perfect, but they kept me functioning at work. Still, my conversational skills suffered, particularly in loud or noisy settings. But just like when I was 12 and coping with my newly reduced eyesight, I had to make do with the solutions I had, and I kept moving along.

STILL MORE ADVENTURE, LESS IMPAIRMENT

When I was 50 years old, in February 2007, I went with a group of fellas from my church, the First Presbyterian Church of River Forest, out to Park City, Utah, to ski. I called ahead to the ski school at Park City and asked if they had any volunteer guides for the visually impaired. They directed me to the National Ability Center, where I arranged to have a guide ski with me the days I would be there.

This would be the first time I'd try skiing with my new hearing aids, and my guide would put the microphone around his or her neck so I could hear verbal commands while we were skiing. I knew my skiing career would be over if I could not accurately hear the voice commands of my guides.

The volunteer guide they arranged for me was a woman named Jennifer Gardner. While she and I were skiing, we talked about my background in skiing, and I told her I'd tried ski racing when I was in my twenties, but I had bombed! I told her it was my plan to someday race again and be successful.

"You're in luck," she told me. "There's a race course at the top of this chairlift, so we'll go down that course."

I told her quite emphatically that I hadn't meant right now or today would be my return to racing, but she guided me with the perfect balance between encouragement and pushiness. We skied the race course several times that day and walked away with a silver NASTAR (National Standard Racing) medal! NASTAR is a national organization that sets up ski racing competitions at resorts across the country.

Well, now I was sure I wouldn't lose skiing because of my hearing loss, and I was hooked on ski racing! For the next three years, 2008, 2009, and 2010, I participated in the NASTAR National Ski Championship and won gold medals— and Jennifer guided me to two of them! She is a very special friend, and we've had several opportunities to ski together since that first trip to Park City.

I've had dozens of ski guides over the many years since my sophomore year in high school. I never would have met any of them if not for my limited eyesight, and I certainly realize I could never ski on my own—just like the volunteer readers who taped all my textbooks were essential to my academic career. I make it a policy to always buy my ski guide coffee and lunch when we ski together, and I tell them directly how meaningful the skiing—and their help—is to me! I'm so thankful for the opportunity their help affords me.

From that first time skiing with Jennifer on, I've felt motivated to push the limits, to determine what I really can and can't do. And each time I succeed at a new adventure, I confirm in my own mind that I am not really handicapped or impaired. I'm simply visually inconvenienced, and now, hard of hearing to boot.

Later in 2009, my brother Pete told me he had participated in a Chicago event called Hustle Up the Hancock, a fundraising event for the Respiratory Health Association of Metropolitan Chicago. Participants raised money by climbing up the 95

floors of the John Hancock Building in downtown Chicago. I was intrigued!

I thought about what challenges such a climb would present to me and decided I should be able to follow Pete up the stairs if he wore one of my bright orange bibs my ski guides used. He and I talked it over, and he agreed to wear a bib that read *Guide* while I wore one that read *Blind Skier*, but I taped over the *Skier* and wrote *Climber* instead!

I found a step-climber exercise machine in the workout room at the office and trained hard during the three months before the climb. The last thing I wanted was to come up short while competing head to head with Pete! (I had not outgrown the competition I've always felt with my twin brother!)

After all this preparation, in February 2010, Pete and I climbed 94 flights of stairs in just over 22 minutes in the Hustle Up the Hancock! The ordeal was even more grueling than I had imagined, but the euphoria and sense of accomplishment at the end was much greater than I had expected too!

In the fall of 2010, JP decided to spend the first semester of his senior year studying overseas—in Australia! Jane and I agreed that Australia was a place we would probably never go to by ourselves, so we made plans to visit JP there in October. We told him to make any and all plans he wanted to during our visit, and when we arrived I learned he had made reservations for the two of us to go bungee jumping! Both Jane and I thought the idea was a bit crazy at first, but I slowly warmed up to it.

JP explained that he had already gone once by himself, and he was sure I could do it just fine. A little while later, as I climbed the stairs to the top of the 260-foot tower to make my jump, I realized my lack of vision was going to be a benefit during this adventure, not a detriment. When I attached the bungee rope to my feet and stepped very slowly and carefully out onto the platform, it looked like I was inside a cloud. I could not at all appreciate how high up I actually was.

I jumped off like I was going into the neighborhood pool, and I felt like I was free-falling only for a second or two before the bungee rope around my legs started to tighten and slow me down. I was confident everything was going to work just fine. As planned, I slowed to a complete stop about ten feet above the ground, but then I was suddenly and unexpectedly shot back up in the air by the bungee cord. And a second later, when I started to slow again, my stomach felt like the bottom had dropped out, and I fell back to earth! This second descent was totally uncontrolled, not at all like my initial dive off the platform.

At that point I began just bouncing up and down, slowing a little bit each time. And I started to laugh uncontrollably. I was still laughing when two guys in a small rowboat came underneath me and raised up a pole for me to grab. After I grabbed it, they pulled me down into the boat, released the bungee cord, and we made our way back to shore.

The sense of accomplishment I felt that day was overwhelming. I had really done it! However, I did not have the feeling that I wanted to do it again right away. Instead I decided I could cross bungee jumping off my to-do list. I was very comfortable saying "one and done" this time.

In January 2011, Pete and I did the "Half Hustle" up the Hancock, which meant going up just 50 flights of stairs. Again, we both had on our orange bibs, which allowed us to move around quite easily without disrupting other climbers.

Right after this Hustle was over, I was contacted by one of the program directors at the Respiratory Health Association of Metropolitan Chicago who told me about a new fundraising event they were going to start in the fall: the Skyline Plunge. The Plunge would offer people a chance to rappel 26 floors down the side of the Wit Hotel, on the northeast corner of Lake and Dearborn streets in downtown Chicago. She told me no prior experience in rappelling was necessary, and it sounded like a blast, so Pete and I signed up.

On the day of the event, we were told to be there half an hour before our "plunge time." During those 30 minutes, the officials explained the mechanics of how the harness and rappelling gear we would be using worked. They showed us the redundant safety precautions in place so there was no way we could be seriously hurt during the Plunge. This information succeeded in taking away my fear of the unknown about rappelling, but it also impressed on me that this was going to take some serious effort.

We took the elevator to the top of the Wit Hotel and were led out on to the totally unfinished roof. We made our way around all kinds of equipment jutting out of the hotel's roof and over to a corner where a large winch had been set up. Looking out at the city from our perch on the 27th floor, I could make out what looked like Marina Towers up the street and across the river. Looking the other way, I could make out the Lake Street el track, which ran right next to the hotel.

Then one of the "Plunge Consultants" fastened the safety line to my harness and tugged at it several times to make sure it was tight and fastened. He told me to turn around and face him, and not to look out or down anymore. He locked the safety line and said, "Okay, slowly shuffle your feet backwards, squeezing the release handle so the line to your safety harness feeds out slowly."

Keeping the line to my harness very tight, I shuffled my feet until I felt the edge of the roof under my heel.

Now the consultant said, "Bend your knees and lock your feet, and lean back to a 45-degree angle, releasing more line slowly."

I did so until my feet were on the corner of the roof and my body was hanging out over the 27-floor drop.

"Now straighten your legs!" the consultant said.

I did so, and my body stretched out over the sidewalk 27 stories below. So now Pete and I ever so slowly released just a little bit of line at a time and began walking backward down the face of the hotel. It took about 25 minutes for us to make our way to the street below.

When I reached the bottom, my feelings rather surprised me: I wanted to go right back up and do it all over again! And I did do the Skyline Plunge three years in a row—2011, 2012, and 2013. The second year I did it with Pete's sons, Zach and Andrew, and the third time with a Kellogg classmate of mine, Ralph Marol.

In 2013, Jane saw an ad in the paper for a place called Drive A Tank. She checked out their website and found that visitors could drive a variety of armored vehicles, fire several different belt-fed machine guns, and even crush a real car with a tank. Seeing how our basement is filled with well over twenty model tanks I've built and painted with the help of my CCTV enlarger, she knew I would love to try that. So she bought me a package for my birthday.

Pete, JP, and I flew to Minneapolis, then drove to Kasota, Minnesota, to the site of Drive A Tank. The experience was beyond my wildest dreams! I would not have even considered putting such a thing on any kind of bucket list, because I couldn't see how it would be possible. However, I told the staff that I was indeed legally blind, and they still made it work. I drove a 35-ton self-propelled artillery gun around a path in the woods. One of their staff tapped me on either my left or right shoulder to indicate which way I needed to direct the vehicle. I also used a two-way headset to receive driving instructions. Then, for the highlight of the day, I climbed into the driver's seat of a 60-ton British Chieftain main battle tank and proceeded to drive it over the top of a Lincoln Continental.

Later that summer, Jane and I went to California to visit JP, who lives there now for his job as he pursues a career in filmmaking. He informed us that he had purchased trapeze lessons for him and me. Of course I thought that was crazy, but I said a prayer and decided I would give it a try. The people at the trapeze school worked with me, and after two hours of practice, I could climb the ladder to the trapeze platform, jump off, swing out, hang by my legs, and finally drop into the net about 20 feet below. It was a real rush! But there was just one thing that bothered me a little: JP and I did all these trapeze things with a class of about ten people—and the whole rest of the class was made up of girls between the ages of 10 and 15!

A year later, in 2014, Jane and I visited JP in Los Angeles again, and I told him I wanted to try the trapeze again. The year before I had seen one person hang by her knees and swing out and catch the hands of another person on another trapeze. I wanted to do that too!

On the day of our lesson, JP and I practiced for a couple

hours, doing the same moves as we had a year before. I finally got brave enough to try to hang by my knees and catch the arms of another person towards the end of our time. And I did it on my last swing of the day!

OH YES, I WAS STILL WORKING

After more than a decade at LaSalle Bank, my career there came to an end when they were bought by Bank of America. Bank of America had legions of people doing the same thing I was doing, so the elimination of my job in Chicago made sense from their big-picture point of view.

There were not many positions in Chicago like the one I had at LaSalle, so I began thinking about other options. One was to move to a smaller investment advisory firm as a registered investment advisor. In the building right next door to LaSalle Bank, there was such a company, the Kovitz Investment Group, and they invited me to join them after I interviewed there in 2008.

My responsibilities were primarily to manage the investments of my clients. I loved it! I felt like I really had come full circle since that time I got so excited when my bank gave me interest as a child. Now I wanted my clients to be excited about me managing their money!

I believe they were, and I continued to enjoy my work in the industry until I retired from the Kovitz Investment Group in 2014. At that point my 35-year career in the wealth management industry came to an end. But even before my retirement, I continued to find plenty of "extracurricular" things to keep me busy.

In the spring of 2015, Jane and I again visited JP in Los Angeles, and he had another new idea for him and myself. One morning, he and I hopped into his car and drove about two hours to a very small airport. We were going to tandem skydive from a small plane!

In a tandem skydive, the novice skydiver hooks himself onto the front of an experienced skydiver, and they leave the plane together. The experienced skydiver has total control of pulling the ripcord and steering the parachute to the perfect landing spot.

Our jumps went off without a hitch, and we even paid to have a photographer jump with us and film the event. It was another great experience, and my list of "been there, done that" items grew another line.

JP has become a great wingman for me, and I'm so grateful that he enjoys finding and planning these adventures for us. As I've said before, each of these crazy accomplishments reminds me that my visual and hearing impairments are only as limiting as I allow them to be. I am thankful for all the challenges in my life—not just the ones that were actually something fun—because of everything they've shown me about God's love, the strength He's given me, and the wonderful people He's placed in my life.

EPILOGUE

I t took the loss of my sight for me to see God's love and the true riches of the blessings He has bestowed upon me. My family was the first blessing in my life, and they remain an enormous blessing to me today. I have realized they are one of the first examples of how God turned my seemingly sad physical hardship into something positive and special.

My high school buddy Dick Mason now lives in Tennessee with his family, and my daughter, Ellie, and his daughter, Ginna Claire, are the same age. They have known each other since they were infants. Without talking to each other, they both applied to Elon University in North Carolina and both got in. They put their names into the freshman class lottery for housing and ended up being suite mates. They lived in a house as roommates for the rest of their college career.

My twin brother and first best friend, Pete, is married and has five children. He and his family live in downtown Chicago now, just 20 minutes away, and we see each other regularly. My three sisters, Karen, JoAnne, and Mary Christine, are all married and have children too. Karen and Mary Christine both live in Downers Grove with their families, and my sister JoAnne lives in Grand Rapids, Michigan—just about an hour from our family cottage. My parents, Hub and Joan, are alive and well and live in Downers Grove, Illinois, just 30 minutes from Jane and me in River Forest.

Each of these people, and so many others who have touched my life, has revealed some aspect of God's love to me. And Jesus has walked beside me all these years, showing His love by guiding me through all the challenges that have arisen.

I was recently flying from Tampa to Chicago, and I had a layover of 90 minutes in Atlanta. I went looking for a place to get a sandwich and saw an area with bright lights and what looked like stools with people sitting down. I walked up to a woman there and asked if I could get a sandwich here.

She said, "Sure, you can sit right over here next to me."

I ordered a sandwich, and the waitress soon brought a basket piled high with chips. I figured the sandwich was under the chips, so I started to feel around in the basket for it. The woman who had helped me to the seat saw what I was doing and told me the sandwich was actually on a separate plate behind the basket.

I thanked her for the help and introduced myself. She said her name was Char, and she was going to Pittsburgh on a job interview. Char had been in the real estate business in Florida for 20 years but had just been let go from her job. We shared stories about having had great jobs, and losing them due to circumstances beyond our control. I thought to myself about the last time I had been between jobs and how scary that felt.

I've only had to find new work twice in my life, and opportunities popped up pretty quickly. I wondered why God had done that for me, and I prayed to myself that God would find Char a job soon too.

It was then time to catch my plane, so I stood up and

thanked her for her help. "Have a great flight and God bless," I told her.

"God bless you too," Char said.

I nodded and said, "He has."

John H. Erickson
johnherickson342@gmail.com
johnherickson.com

Printed in the United States
By Bookmasters